Cambridge Eler

Elements in the Archaeology
edited by
Manuel Fernández-G
University of Edinburgh
Bettina Arnold
University of Wisconsin–Milwaukee

C000082746

DIGITAL INNOVATIONS IN EUROPEAN ARCHAEOLOGY

Kevin Garstki
University of Wisconsin-Oshkosh

European Association
of Archaeologists

CAMBRIDGE
UNIVERSITY PRESS

CAMBRIDGE
UNIVERSITY PRESS

University Printing House, Cambridge CB2 8BS, United Kingdom

One Liberty Plaza, 20th Floor, New York, NY 10006, USA

477 Williamstown Road, Port Melbourne, VIC 3207, Australia

314–321, 3rd Floor, Plot 3, Splendor Forum, Jasola District Centre,
New Delhi – 110025, India

79 Anson Road, #06–04/06, Singapore 079906

Cambridge University Press is part of the University of Cambridge.

It furthers the University's mission by disseminating knowledge in the pursuit of
education, learning, and research at the highest international levels of excellence.

www.cambridge.org
Information on this title: www.cambridge.org/9781108744126
DOI: 10.1017/9781108881425

© Kevin Garstki 2020

This publication is in copyright. Subject to statutory exception
and to the provisions of relevant collective licensing agreements,
no reproduction of any part may take place without the written
permission of Cambridge University Press.

First published 2020

A catalogue record for this publication is available from the British Library.

ISBN 978-1-108-74412-6 Paperback
ISSN 2632-7058 (online)
ISSN 2632-704X (print)

Additional resources for this publication at www.cambridge.org/garstki

Cambridge University Press has no responsibility for the persistence or accuracy of
URLs for external or third-party internet websites referred to in this publication
and does not guarantee that any content on such websites is, or will remain,
accurate or appropriate.

Digital Innovations in European Archaeology

Elements in the Archaeology of Europe

DOI: 10.1017/9781108881425
First published online: November 2020

Kevin Garstki
University of Wisconsin-Oshkosh

Author for correspondence: Kevin Garstki, garstkik@uwosh.edu

Abstract: European archaeologists in the last two decades have worked to integrate a wide range of emerging digital tools to enhance the recording, analysis, and dissemination of archaeological data. These techniques have expanded and altered the data collected by archaeologists as well as their interpretations. At the same time archaeologists have expanded the capabilities of using these data on a large scale, across platforms, regions, and time periods, utilising new and existing digital research infrastructures to enhance the scale of data used for archaeological interpretations. This Element discusses some of the most recent, innovative uses of these techniques in European archaeology at different stages of archaeological work. In addition to providing an overview of some of these techniques, it critically assesses these approaches and outlines the recent challenges to the discipline posed by self-reflexive use of these tools and advocacy for their open use in cultural heritage preservation and public engagement.

Keywords: digital archaeology, public archaeology, open science, data archiving, 3D modelling

© Kevin Garstki 2020

ISBNs: 9781108744126 (PB), 9781108881425 (OC)
ISSNs: 2632-7058 (online), ISSN 2632-704X (print)

Contents

1 Introduction

1.1 Introduction to the Volume

European archaeology in the 21st century is a digital discipline. It has been argued that 'we are all digital archaeologists' (Morgan and Eve 2012, 523). Isto Huvila has even gone so far as to suggest that 'there is no digital archaeology and no digital society. There is merely archaeology and society, and the digital is a facet of a particular set of technologies and a cultural phenomenon that permeates contemporary existence both when it is present and when it is absent' (2018, 1).

Information collected from fieldwork is either collected digitally or immediately converted from analogue to digital form. Visual archaeological data are all collected digitally, from digital photographs to laser scans. The ways data are managed, curated, and disseminated are essentially all conducted through a digital interface. These digital platforms have changed the way archaeologists consider their obligations to preserve and increase the availability of cultural heritage, and have provided new avenues for archaeology to continue to be a more ethically minded and publicly oriented discipline. However, with all of these changes, the impact that the rapid development of digital technologies has had on European archaeology is difficult to assess because it is so pervasive.

New digital techniques for recording and visualising data retain the underlying principles of archaeology; excavations are conducted in much the same way as they have been over the last half century, spatial data are recorded and collected as they have been, and artefacts are still visually represented. The major changes over the last decade or so have been the platforms, methods, and tools used to record and collect these data. What has also changed is the way archaeologists think about archaeological data and how archaeology is practiced in the 21st century, a century largely defined by digital technology.

This Element will trace these advances and applications in digital technology in European archaeology and how they have transformed the way archaeology is practiced. Various techniques and applications will be viewed through the lens of broad disciplinary change, as archaeologists have moved through stages of initial experimentation to critical assessment of the disciplinary impact that digital tools have on the field of archaeology in Europe. Some of the most recent, innovative uses of these techniques by European archaeologists in different stages of archaeological work, the challenges to the discipline for self-reflexive use of these tools, and their open use in cultural heritage preservation and public engagement will all be discussed.

Obviously when writing about a theme as exceptionally broad as the use of digital technologies in archaeology, no single aspect can be explored completely nor can all aspects be covered. This Element provides a critical review of how some of the most recent digital innovations in archaeological practice are impacting European archaeology today. As such, individual case studies and projects will be highlighted that emphasise certain important characteristics of this 'digital revolution'. There is, of course, no way to properly acknowledge all the work conducted throughout the continent, but this Element will act as a starting point for those less familiar with these techniques, while providing a critical look at the impact of digital technology on archaeology.

1.2 Mainframes and Databanks

Although recent digital innovations have altered archaeological practice in the past two decades, threads of these digital approaches have been present since the 1960s; the 'digital revolution' is now fully matured. Archaeological computing can be traced back half a century to the first use of computers in the 1960s and 1970s (Richards and Ryan 1985). Prior to the widespread use of computer-based applications on archaeological data, following World War II to the mid-1960s, archaeology was a fast-emerging field of quantitative science, developing statistical and graphical approaches that have become the foundation of the modern processing of archaeological data (Djindjian 2009). After some analyses were conducted by using machine-sorted punch cards, pioneering archaeologist Jean-Claude Gardin, with Peter Ihm, were the first to use electronic processing for an archaeological application in 1958 or 1959 (Cowgill 1967; Dallas 2016). At that point computer mainframes were limited to well-funded institutions that could support the air-conditioned, purpose-built facilities necessary to maintain the computers (Lock 2003, 9). The initial foci were information retrieval, statistical computing, data processing, and modelling (Richards and Ryan 1985, 3). Unsurprisingly, the early developments in computing in archaeology were established alongside changes in theoretical approaches in the discipline, such as processual thinking, quantification, neo-evolutionary schema, and scientific approaches (Chenhall 1968; Lock 2003, 8). Gardin's influence on the development of archaeological computing has been unfortunately downplayed (Dallas 2016), but his foundational thinking on archaeological classification and description structured much of the early work in archaeological computing and even permeates some of the most recent developments (Gardin 1971; 1980). Following the work of Gardin and others, the first major advancements in computing in the discipline came in the form of computer-based statistics, specifically multi-variate statistics that drew on a strong European tradition of culture history.[1] Possibly the most illustrative of this early quantitative focus on computer applications in archaeology is Doran and Hodson's 1975 *Mathematics and Computers in Archaeology.*

In the late 1960s and early 1970s Robert Chenhall was an early proponent of utilising the storage capacity of computers to aid in archaeological research. As he noted, 'the computer seems to offer the most logical extension of human mental facilities yet devised, if it can be utilised effectively' (1971, 159). Even in this early period researchers recognised the benefits that computers could provide, supplementing the knowledge capacity of written documents and reports. Unfortunately, the early attempts at creating widespread archaeological databanks did not live up to expectations due to the limits of hardware and storage, lack of institutional support, and the absence of standardisation in what types of archaeological data should be stored (Chenhall 1971; Scholtz and Chenhall 1976).

It was this push towards the use of archaeological databanks that led to the first Archaeological Data Bank Conference in 1971 at the University of Arkansas Museum, US (Watrall 2016). The concept behind this conference, organising archaeologists to discuss the use of computers in research as it related to storing and preserving data, was also foundational for the beginning of the Computer Applications and Quantitative Methods in Archaeology (CAA)[2] conference in 1973, organised in Birmingham, UK.[3] The CAAs have continued to this day with an ever-growing membership.

The early visions for large-scale archaeological computing have begun to be realised. Statistical computing and computational modelling remain important aspects of archaeological research in Europe and computers have provided necessary avenues for the storage, curation, and preservation of digital archaeological data. The push for standardised databanks in the late 1960s and 1970s is finally coming to fruition. Data archiving services such as the Archaeology Data Service (ADS) or the Digital Archaeological Record (tDAR), or country-specific archives such as the Data Archiving and Data Service (DANS) in the Netherlands or the digital services of the German Archaeological Institute (iDAI), are the descendants of databanks proposed in these early years of archaeological computing.[4] Furthermore, larger international digital infrastructures such as ARIADNE and Europeana are connecting data across platforms

---

[1] Although not all uses of statistical methods in archaeology were appropriate or well done (Thomas 1978).

[2] https://caa-international.org/about/history

[3] See this video on some of the history of the CAA from participants. https://www.sms.cam.ac.uk/media/1357554

[4] See Section 3 for detailed descriptions of these archives.

and repositories, using standardised schema such as CIDOC CRM to address the weakness that Chenhall lamented in the 1970s. As data storage and archiving become a larger focus in Europe, archaeologists are also working to avoid another digital dark age, when data was lost due to corrupted CDs, unreadable file types, changing software, or obsolete hardware (see Jeffrey 2012). Projects such as the COST ACTION 'Saving European Archaeology from the Digital Dark Age' (SEADDA) aim to avoid a further loss of data by developing a series of best practices for the preservation, dissemination, and reuse of archaeological data in Europe.

Although recent digital innovations have altered archaeological practice in the past two decades, the seeds of these digital approaches were planted in the 1960s; the 'revolution' is far from its early stages. In fact, Gary Lock has suggested that the 'digital revolution' actually began just after these early appearances of archaeological computing, with the widespread arrival of the microprocessor in the late 1970s (2003, 10). The shrinking of processors in the early 1970s allowed a move from large mainframe computers and eventually provided the foundation for desktop computing; by the late 1970s microcomputers had become a very real part of archaeological research. The shift in hardware also accompanied a disciplinary shift away from the 'quantitative revolution in archaeology', as Djindjian (2009) terms it, of the mid-1960s to the mid-1970s, to applications for wider use by archaeologists. Computer accessibility continued to increase over the next four decades, leading to the current digital landscape. In this sense archaeology is not at the beginning stages of a disciplinary revolution but well into it (see the historiographic discussions in Djindjian 2009; 2019 and Moscati 2019). This is precisely why in the editorial for the Digital Archaeology special issue of *Frontiers in Digital Humanities* Andre Costopoulos takes the firm stance that archaeology has been digital for forty years (2016). The role of computers in archaeology is not a recent revolution but one that has been steadily developing for decades. At the same time the most recent techniques being adopted by archaeologists, many of which have only become possible due to the exponential growth in computing power, are greatly impacting archaeology in this century.

1.3 Rethinking Archaeology

The growth of these technologies is evident, but what underlies the adoption of these tools is a discipline-wide re-evaluation of the way archaeology is practiced. As Jeremy Huggett suggests in his blog, 'Digital Archaeology should be a means of rethinking archaeology, rather than simply a series of methodologies and techniques' (2016). The challenges that 21st century archaeologists face have not arisen with the adoption of digital tools but have been here the whole time. The transition to these tools has only highlighted, and in some cases exacerbated, these disciplinary dilemmas. This Element will address how different types of digital tools are allowing us to re-think some of these challenges.

Section 2 presents how the role of digital data collection in fieldwork has facilitated significant methodological shifts in the way excavations and surveys are conducted. From mobile digital recording devices to laser scanning to computational photogrammetry, digital tools have been adopted at a rapid pace over the last decade. However, accompanying these adoptions are critiques about the change in excavation methodologies, including the potential for these digital tools to 'de-skill' archaeologists (Caraher 2013; 2016), or the worry that our growing reliance on digital techniques exacerbates a technological fetishism that seems to persist in the discipline.

Section 3 outlines how recent techniques to visualise cultural heritage have been quickly adopted for archaeological research. Digital 3D artefacts, Reflectance Transformation Imaging (RTI), and virtual reconstructions of sites and buildings have all expanded the way archaeologists and non-professionals experience the archaeological record. Their expanding use has also brought to the fore questions of authenticity and authority, questions that in the past were mainly applicable to physical casts, replicas, and illustrated reconstructions.

Echoing larger trends in the sciences and humanities, archaeology has expanded its goals regarding open and accessible data. Section 4 describes how this move attempts to address long-held challenges in archaeological research: how to preserve and curate data for the long term, how to make data useful with other regionally distinct datasets, and how to make these data available to researchers and other stakeholders. Wide-reaching international projects, some funded by the European Union (EU) Commission, have worked to standardise many aspects of archaeological preservation by establishing interconnected digital infrastructures to communicate between datasets using shared ontologies.[5] Additionally, ambitious archiving schema aim to provide access to digital archaeological data for decades to come.

Section 5 outlines some of the outcomes of the widespread use of digital platforms for archaeological research that provide opportunities to include various stakeholders in the archaeological endeavour. Although archaeology has long attempted to be a public discipline, 'digital archaeology of the 21st

---

[5] In information science, ontologies refer to the structure, formal naming of categories and concepts, and representation of a unified domain of data.

century is necessarily a public archaeology' (Graham et al. 2019). Social media platforms increase not only the reach of archaeological research, but they also create opportunities for interactions between non-archaeologists and archaeologists. In addition, digital tools allow more significant input from those outside traditional disciplinary bounds to shape archaeological research and the ways it impacts communities.

The Element ends by exploring how newly emerging digital approaches may shape European archaeology in the future. The ever-expanding fields of 'Big Data' analysis and machine learning may have drastic implications for the practice of archaeology, moving archaeology further into a data-driven paradigm shift. The accelerated move towards a fully digital discipline also reminds us that we are participating in a larger, digital world, and as a result contribute to global issues of sustainability. Future directions in European archaeology cannot be isolated from international socio-politics but are situated firmly within it.

2 Digital Data Collection in the Field

In a discipline that is prone to conservatism in its methods, the move away from analogue data collection has certainly seemed rapid. But although the transition to primary data collection in digital formats may appear to have happened overnight in archaeology, in truth this process has been accelerating over the last two decades. We are seeing a significant shift to born-digital data collection in European archaeology. The 'born digital' concept is ubiquitous in archaeological discourse at the moment. In the recent volume *Mobilizing the Past for a Digital Future: The Potential of Digital Archaeology* (Averett et al. 2016), a publication focused on new digital collection methods in the field, the term appears forty-three times.[6] The term refers to data that are collected in digital form, never being recorded with a pen and paper but only existing in a digital space. This contrasts with information that was originally collected in analogue form and was then transferred to a digital medium (i.e., digitisation). The term likely has its origin in the mid-to-late 1990s in library contexts, due in part to the digitisation of printed text (versus computer-generated text that could be digitally archived directly). This concept gained a foothold in archaeological research in the early 2000s (e.g., Hopkinson and Winters 2003), due to an increased reliance on digital photography and digital databases for immediate data collection.

The increased use of the term suggests a wider trend in the discipline for transferring documentation of landscapes, sites, and excavation practices directly into a computational environment. The pace of straight-to-digital

---

[6] This includes a few uses of 'digitally born'.

recording practices has only intensified in the past decade, when mobile tablets, drones, and 3D data-capturing technologies have become less expensive and more user-friendly. At the moment many excavation projects in Europe are generating most of their data with digital techniques. It is safe to assume all projects are using digital cameras to capture visual data, but a growing number use some or all of the following practices to gather data without putting pen to paper.

2.1 Mobile Recording in the Field

Archaeological field collection methods vary widely throughout the world. Mary Leighton's (2015) important comparison of practices in archaeological fieldwork highlighted the lack of standardisation in data collection methods, as well as the practices employed by different archaeological projects. For this reason, it is difficult to generalise about recording practices throughout Europe, in private versus academic contexts, or through the myriad archaeological contexts (single-context versus stratigraphic excavations). However, it appears clear that in the last decade the use of mobile devices for field recording has expanded significantly. In many cases digital devices equipped with proprietary or bespoke software act as the main source of data documentation (see Averett et al. 2016 for numerous examples). A few benefits are clear: by removing the process of analogue recording and subsequent transcription in a digital format, one opportunity for error to creep in is also removed; discrete datasets such as past excavation data, images, maps, and artefact data can all be accessible at once in the field to aid in archaeological choices; one can make use of the different features of the devices such as built-in photography or GPS for enhanced documentation.

The types of software used for digital recording also vary considerably. Although some projects rely on proprietary database systems like FileMaker, others utilise the growing number of generalised open-source platforms for mobile recording (Dufton 2016; Sobotkova et al. 2016). ARK (The Archaeological Recording Kit)[7] developed by LP Archaeology, for example, is a web-based framework for data collection, storage, and visualisation which can be customised for different projects. Another, ArcheoPackPro!, developed within the CONPRA(Contributing the Preventive Archaeology)[8] project, communicates with otherwise independent modular systems to exchange different types of data (Tasić 2017a). Web applications such as ARK and PKapp (Fee 2013) do not require Internet access, something often limited when working in the field, but do need a local network from which to access the necessary web

---

[7] https://ark.lparchaeology.com/about/   [8] Described in Tasić 2017a

technologies. There are benefits and drawbacks to any of the recording solutions projects choose to use. On the one hand, applications like FileMaker may be limited in the amount of customisation possible but there is technical support in case of issues. On the other hand, free and open-source software (FOSS) allows greater flexibility at less or no cost (Edwards and Wilson 2015; Ducke 2012), but maintenance can become an issue if there is no dedicated 'tech person' on staff. Open-source programs also increase the possibilities for reproducing research and avoid relying on institutional software choices and licenses (Ducke 2015).

Early examples of born-digital recording often occurred in large, well-funded projects around the Mediterranean (see Walldrodt 2016). As the technologies became more easily accessible, the use of mobile devices and field laptop computers varied from project to project. Some chose to make use of tablets to enhance specific aspects of excavation recording like field notebooks (Gordon et al. 2016), while others moved to a more integrative approach to data collection, management, and access (Motz and Carrier 2013; Motz 2016). Excavation projects have taken this approach to another level by integrating mobile context recording in the form of field notes and forms directly into database structures, while also integrating other forms of born-digital field recording techniques like computational photogrammetry (López et al. 2016; Roosevelt et al. 2015; Sikora and Kittel 2018). The aim of these approaches is to completely connect all data collected from the field. Digital data collection on mobile devices helps with this by standardising data collection in the form of integrated databases and providing efficient connections to other types of data. In theory, mobile field recording helps not only with efficiency in data collection but enhances the usability of those data out of the field. However, as discussed in Section 2.3, efficiency in data collection raises many questions about archaeological epistemology and the future envisioned for the discipline.

2.2 Recording in Three Dimensions

The use of three-dimensional recording technology, such as laser scanners and computational photogrammetry, has become increasingly common in archaeology over the last decade for the documentation of sites and landscapes. Range-based systems, such as laser scanners or structure light scanners, rely on the capture of absolute surface geometry, whereas image-based systems, such as computational photogrammetry, create relative spatial distances on the model (Remondino and El-Hakim 2006). Laser scanning refers to 'any technology which accurately and repeatedly measures distance, based on a precise measurement of time, and aggregates these measurements into a collection of coordinates' (Opitz 2013, 13). Airborne laser scanning (ALS), often used interchangeably with the term LiDAR (Light Detection And Ranging), began to grow in prominence beginning in the early 2000s as a result of innovations in equipment, data processing, software, and GPS technologies that significantly lowered the costs of these approaches (Opitz 2013). The two most common methods that laser scanners employ to measure distance either record the time it takes for a laser pulse to return to the instrument that emitted it (Time of Flight [TOF]) or calculate distance from the instrument by measuring the phase shift between the emitted and received continuous laser beam (Phase Shift Scanner). Most ALS scanners use TOF technology for recording their calculations (Bennett 2014; Opitz 2013). Terrestrial laser scanners (TLS) began to be used in archaeology around the same time as ALS systems, focused on the site, feature, and object-level documentation (Lercari 2016).

The amount and pace at which these surveying techniques have taken hold in archaeology cannot be understated. Entire countries in Europe now have complete LiDAR coverage, and often these governmental survey data are freely available. Slovenia, for example, has 3D landscape data available for the whole nation. The benefits of ALS for archaeological and topographic survey and remote sensing are obvious; large swaths of landscapes can be surveyed, it provides the ability to visualise features without the hinderance of vegetation, and the high resolution provided by laser scanning has truly opened new worlds for archaeology. But we can also see the benefit that this technique brings to conceptualisations of landscape, especially as it relates to the archaeological record (Mlekuž 2013; Risbøl 2013). LiDAR-derived data provides an opportunity for sites and archaeological features to be viewed as parts of the wider topographic and archaeological landscape rather than as discrete entities. And although this is not an approach unique to ALS, the seemingly straightforward visualisations that are created with these data emphasise the usefulness of this conceptualisation of landscape.

A recent example of the potential for ALS to reimagine an archaeological landscape is the examination of an Iron Age hillfort landscape around Knežak, Slovenia, by Laharnar et al. (2019). The application of ALS-derived data, through a data-specific processing approach, illuminated the complex spatial and temporal landscape of this region. Using these data, the authors were able to identify groups of cairnfields, linear earthworks, enclosures, and hollow ways that were possibly built and used largely contemporaneously as the hillforts (Figure 1). These newly identified features demonstrate that thinking of sites as discrete entities restricts possible reconstructions; the linear earthworks identified through ALS possibly acted as boundaries between hillforts, and pathways extended out from the hillfort at Gradišče above Knežak to create an intra- and

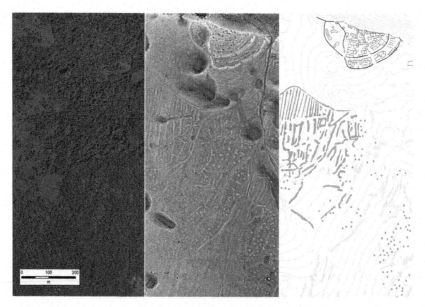

Figure 1 Gradišče above Knežak, Slovenian Iron Age hillfort. Left: aerial photography. Centre: visualisation of processed airborne LiDAR data. Right: the archaeological interpretation. Only the hillfort ramparts (black) were known before airborne LiDAR data was analysed. (Created by Edisa Lozić)

inter-site network (Laharnar et al. 2019, 252). The proper utilisation of ALS-derived data opens new possibilities to reimagine landscape and prehistoric lifeways, as this project demonstrates.

The robustness and durability of these 3D data are also demonstrated by the continuous discovery and reusability of long-running projects. Corns and Shaw (2013) outlined a broad endeavour in Ireland, funded by a combination the National Monuments Service and the Heritage Council, to capture high-resolution 3D survey data for two UNESCO World Heritage Sites and two significant royal sites. Parts of the processed data from these projects can still be viewed online.[9] And although the data derived from these ALS projects have provided enticing and publicly engaging relief-shaded DSMs,[10] the most inter-esting aspect of an otherwise standard (albeit wide-ranging) 3D landscape project is the length of time that the data continue to be used for new research discoveries. A good example is the particularly robust dataset created for the Brú na Boinne landscape. New discoveries and reinterpretations of the ALS data continue to be made even though the data were captured more than

---

[9] https://dcenr.maps.arcgis.com/apps/webappviewer/index.html?id=b7c4b0e763964070 ad69bf8c1572c9f5
[10] Digital Surface Model.

a decade ago, and are now being combined with other methods of remote sensing to come to new realisations (Corns and Shaw 2013; Davis et al. 2013; Davis et al. 2019).

Despite the apparent usefulness of these 3D data for landscape survey and site/ feature identification, ALS data are still not used as extensively as one would expect. A major reason for this is their large size and limited accessibility. Due to the highly detailed nature of the data collected via ALS, the size of files and the computing power required to process the data are immense. These issues are being minimised in part due to the development of personal computing technology and the lowering of software prices, albeit slowly. An additional issue that has stymied the potential of landscape ALS data are the limits to sharing or publishing these data, specifically the processed data, which includes full para- and metadata[11] (Štular, forthcoming). Until institutionally supported platforms or venues to host wide-ranging LiDAR-derived data become more prevalent, the reach of the technology may continue to be limited to a smaller subset of archaeological contexts.

To mitigate some of the issues represented by aerial and terrestrial laser scanning a different 3D data-capturing technique, known colloquially as photogrammetry, has exploded in popularity in archaeology. Photogrammetry is not a new tool or technology, as the term simply refers to the extraction of three-dimensional measurements from two-dimensional images, and it has existed nearly as long as photography. Archaeologists have long been making use of 2D photogrammetry for simply rectification or orthorectification (Štuhec and Zachar 2017). The principle is based loosely upon our own stereoscopic vision, in which points on the original scene are calculated by using overlapping images. This technique evolved over time from an analogue process to a computer-aided one, where mathematical algorithms are calculated by a computer program, and a graphical user interface (GUI) largely controls the photogrammetric analysis (Remondino and El-Hakim 2006). The technique widely used by archaeologists today should more accurately be called computational, digital, or automated photogrammetry, highlighting the computer's role in the final product.

Computational photogrammetry is an image-based modelling technique that relies on passive sensors (the camera) to gather spatial data (see Remondino 2014 for more detailed explanation). Many archaeologists utilising this technique are now using Agisoft's Metashape software (formally Photoscan), although other open-source options are available such as Bundler and Patch Based Multi-View Stereo (Green et al. 2014). Agisoft utilises a common technique for photogrammetric scene construction called Structure from Motion

---

[11] Metadata are data that provide information about data, such as keywords or archaeological context. Paradata are data describing the process by which the data were created, such as what type of camera was used for a photograph.

(SfM)[12] and Multi View Stereo (MVS) for interpolating a denser point cloud after the photographs are aligned and common features are identified (Sapirstein 2018, 34). It should be noted that this SfM and MVS package is also utilised by other automated photogrammetric software (Štuhec and Zachar 2017, 38–42). It is therefore also acceptable to refer to the process of computational photogrammetry as SfM, although this simplifies the productive process.

Once a standard image-capturing workflow is established, the technique is readily integrated into excavation practices, complementing or even replacing traditional field documentation methods like photography and mapping (however, see the discussion in Section 2.3 for arguments against this replacement). The underlying strategy for this data capture method is that each part of the surface that one wishes to document must be visible in at least two overlapping images and that the images must be taken from different physical locations (Figure 2). This is, of course, a simplistic description of the technique, and for maximum accuracy, resolution, and image detail, many other factors must be

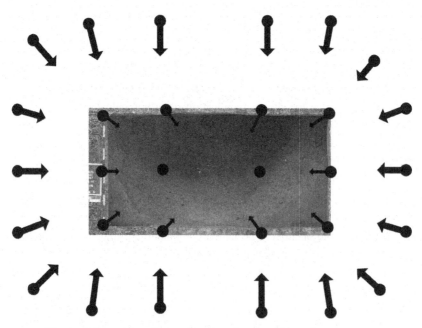

Figure 2 Example of how photographs should be taken to create
a photogrammetric model of an excavation trench. Dots represent the location
of the photographer and arrows represent the direction of the photograph; the
downward angle of the photograph is not illustrated here.

---

[12] This includes an algorithm similar to Scale-Invariant Feature Transform (SIFT), a computer vision algorithm for feature detection, to identify shared features across 2D images.

taken into account including image quality, photographic variables (such as focal length, aperture, ISO), image processing, and use of georeferenced markers (Sapirstein 2016; Štuhec and Zachar 2017). After initial data capture and image processing, the workflow within the photogrammetric software is typically consistent: SfM locates the images in space in relation to one another, in part by identifying shared measurements – this creates a 'point cloud', which is a group of 3D measurements in space on the surface of the scene. After creating a more densely packed point cloud, these points are connected into a 'mesh' which approximates the surface of the original scene. Finally, an amalgam of the images (a 'phototexture') is created that is aligned to the mesh so that the digital model looks like the original scene (Figure 3).

These techniques have been used frequently in various archaeological contexts across Europe. Aerial photogrammetry, utilising photographs taken by unmanned aerial vehicles (UAVs), has been used to document larger landscapes (e.g., Opitz and Cowley 2013b; Roosevelt 2014; Smith et al. 2014; Wernke et al. 2016) and close-range photogrammetry is becoming a ubiquitous recording tool on excavations and for historic architectural recording (e.g., Demesticha et al. 2014; de Reu et al. 2014; Dell'Unto 2014; Forte 2014; Howland et al. 2014; Hill et al. 2014; Olson et al. 2013; Opitz 2015; Roosevelt et al. 2015; Sapirstein 2016; Sapirstein and Murray 2017; Smith and Levy 2012, 2014; Štuhec and Zachar 2015; Zachar and Horňák 2017). The low financial entry point to photogrammetry has made it an ideal technique for archaeologists, who are often working on a shoe-string budget (Kersten and Lindstaedt 2012). Most archaeological projects are already equipped with a digital SLR camera and

Figure 3 Top left: aligned photos taken for computational photogrammetry, represented by the squares. Top right: point cloud. Bottom left: mesh. Bottom right: mesh with accompanying phototexture.

most of the necessary software licenses for image processing are open access or available at steeply reduced educational discounts.

With the proliferation of computational photogrammetry in archaeology we may ask the question, What do we do with these 3D models of sites and features once we have created them? Ironically, perhaps the most useful (or at least most widely used) product of these 3D visualisations is the 2D images that can be generated from them. Plan view and section view orthorectified images can be produced from these 3D models, since the models are geo-rectified to a coordinate system during the data collection and processing phases (Figure 4). Although basic rectification of images was conducted using the first CAD and GIS software, the automation of this process has increased significantly with computational photogrammetry. In the last decade researchers have demonstrated the error rate is hardly present in many of these models, if done correctly (de Reu et al. 2013; Olson et al. 2013; Quartermaine et al. 2014; Sapirstein 2016). Accurate orthophotos can be uploaded directly into a GIS and mapped onto without the need for hand-

Figure 4 Top left: two views of a 3D model of the sanctuary at Athienou-*Malloura*, Cyprus. Top right: 2D orthophoto created from the 3D model. Bottom: 2D sections made of the 3D model.

drawn maps (Figure 5). Of course, the complete replacement of field drawing by digital recording systems has been viewed with scepticism by a number of scholars.

Aside from the 2D products that accompany 3D photogrammetric models there is also potential for making great use of the 3D models themselves. Mapping can be completed in three dimensions on the model directly in a program like ESRI ArcScene because the models are georeferenced. For example, Wihelmson and Dell'Unto (2015) demonstrated the usefulness of this approach, applying 3D mapping to their analysis and reconstruction of burials, employing what they term 'Virtual Taphonomy'. In their case study the authors relied on the linking of varied bioarchaeological, spatial, and archaeological data in a single geo-database that aided in their analysis of the complex stratigraphic and taphonomic context at the Migration Period site of Sandby borg, Öland, Sweden. Furthermore, researchers can make use of these photogrammetric models for volumetric analyses, which represent a new way to think about the three-dimensional spaces we excavate (Jaklič et al. 2015; Roosevelt et al. 2015).

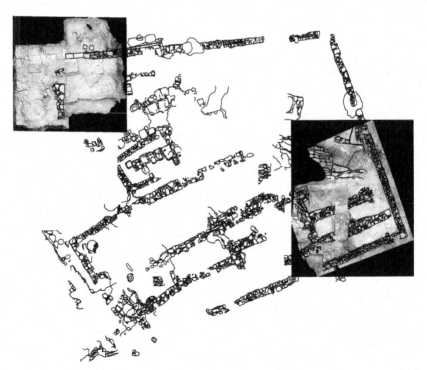

Figure 5 Orthophotos uploaded in a GIS, mapping directly from the georeferenced image.

However, despite of the potential for 3D models created with computational photogrammetry to expand the analytical possibilities of digital field recording (see Landeschi et al. 2015; 2016; Piccoli 2016; Wihelmson and Dell'Unto 2015), these approaches are still limited. The work pioneered by Jensen and Aarhus University represents one way forward (Jensen 2018a). By establishing a 3D documentation workflow from the onset of excavations at Alken Enge, Denmark (AD 200–500), they were able to transition the resultant 3D data into post-field research workflows. The eventual research output of this process provides a model for the integration of 3D data into robust data analysis. A web-based 3D viewer and connected database, Archeao,[13] combines 3D models either created on site using SfM or virtual reconstructions with a PostgreSQL database that contains all of the site, feature, and object information (Jensen 2018a; 2018b). Isolating individual entities from a 3D model extends its utility beyond being simply a visualisation aide by linking it to feature/object data. This type of purpose-built platform may be currently out of reach for most archaeological projects or institutions, but it does provide a standard for which to aim in the effort to completely integrate 3D data into robust archaeological analysis.

One widespread use of the 3D photogrammetric models themselves is in the reconstruction of excavations. As projects continue to integrate this field-recording technique into their archaeological workflow, we are left with detailed three-dimensional, high-resolution reminders of how the excavation took place. It is difficult to quantify how models such as these can help in the understanding of an archaeological site and their increasing role in the construction of archaeological knowledge (Dell'Unto 2018; Garstki et al. 2018). But anyone who has worked with legacy archaeological data can attest that 3D models would be a helpful addition. The three-dimensional spatial environment that they allow us to engage with is arguably a significant improvement over the approximated three-dimensions that can be reconstructed using 2D plan and section maps (Video 1).

Digital 3D models of archaeological or heritage scenes also lend themselves to sharing with other researchers and the public, due in part to their 'cool factor'. A few platforms, such as Sketchfab, have arisen that provide places to easily upload and access 3D archaeological models. Although the details of this growing phenomenon will be elaborated on in Section 3, access to these models is providing an expanding community a place to interact directly with archaeological contexts and finds. In some cases, projects are aimed at fully integrating 3D photogrammetric models with their interpretation of the text, as seen in the publication *A Mid-Republican House from Gabii* (2016) (see discussion in Opitz 2018). Integrated texts like these make use of 3D models as objects of

---

[13] https://archaeo.au.dk/

Video 1 Video of the interaction with a photogrammetric model of a sculptural deposit mid-excavation at the sanctuary at Athienou-*Malloura*, Cyprus. Video available at www.cambridge.org/garstki

archaeological knowledge that can aid directly in storytelling and historical reconstructions. Along these same lines, photogrammetric models can also be utilised for educational purposes, to enhance student or public engagement with the archaeological record at a scale unavailable through traditional media (Di Giuseppantonio Di Franco et al. 2012; Forte 2014; Garstki et al. 2019).

2.3 Critiques and Caveats

The move to an all-digital recording strategy for both visual documentation and for excavation data has caused disagreement among archaeologists as to the consequences of this methodological shift, specifically the potential impact on traditional archaeological epistemology. Roosevelt et al. (2015) posit that the shift to an all-digital recording practice in archaeological excavations demonstrates a paradigmatic change in the discipline, one where not only do the methods of recording change but so do the spatial conceptions of excavations, to one of three-dimensional volume. The proposal of a paradigm shift has been resisted for a number of reasons, such as the suggestion that these conceptions have always been a part of archaeology (e.g., Gordon et al. 2016). Yet, regardless of the terminology used to describe this methodological transition, it is undeniable that a move to completely (or mostly) born-digital recording practices impacts the processes by which we create archaeological data and knowledge.

However, as often seems to be the case with archaeology's adoption of a new technique, mobile recording, ALS, and other 3D data capture present great potential for a technological 'black box', in Latour's sense of the term (1987). As the technology becomes complex, it is put inside a 'black box' where the only concern is the input and the output. And with success and efficiency comes an uncritical acceptance of its work. Few people other than the specialists in this 3D data capture technique recognize the significant processing and input that goes into the visualisation of 3D landscape data using laser scanners. As Opitz and Cowley (2013a, 6) highlight, 'terrain models, like any models, are constructs and often riddled with unspoken assumptions'. Data derived from ALS need to be processed and interpreted to contribute any meaningful archaeological information, although at times this interpretation is not completely transparent (Doneus and Kühteiber 2013). There is always a danger of misrepresentation of archaeological features, especially if the data collected were not intended for an archaeological project (Bennett 2014). Access to new visualisation platforms and processing algorithms offer more opportunities for archaeologists to use these techniques, opening these tools to a wider user base. However, this also has the potential for some to use the data without fully understanding their underlying structures. As with any new technique applied to archaeological contexts, the use of airborne and terrestrial laser scanning must be used with a critical understanding of its methods and their potential impact on the data and subsequent interpretation.

Digital field recording practices like mobile devices or computational photogrammetry bring with them significant benefits, but also major questions. Some possible benefits are that more data can be collected, in more standardised ways, often in more efficient ways. The increase in data standardisation that accompanies the shift to digital recording fills an important gap in archaeological thinking. Traditionally, data have not been considered in the long term after being collected – people do not inherently 'think like databases' nor has there been an eye towards how archaeological data can be reused after initial collection and use in primary research (Faniel et al. 2018). Standardisation provides more robust futures for archaeological data: the ability to connect disparate datasets to reuse archaeological data (see Section 4). Not only does gathering more digital data benefit archaeological work in the moment (we cannot put back the dirt and dig it again) but it fits into larger-scale thinking that includes the future use of those data. There is no excuse not to consider the future in archaeological practice (Garstki 2017; Witmore 2009), even if we do not always get those futures right. But we must also question what information is lost in standardisation. A reliance on an overly structured classification schema forces an excavator to make either/or choices in the field, resulting in a loss of nuance and possible variability. The increased use of standard digital tick boxes or drop-down fields ignores an important aspect of interpretation at the trowel's edge. In an effort to record more information more quickly, do we miss out on the otherwise hard-to-quantify information of an excavation?

William Caraher has introduced the idea of 'slow archaeology' as a critique of the ethos of efficiency that often accompanies the shift to digital recording strategies in the field (2013; 2016). As he suggests, 'the goal of slow archaeology is to recognise the particular emphasis on efficiency, economy, and standardisation in digital practices within the larger history of scientific and industrial knowledge production in archaeology' (Caraher 2016, 423). Indeed, the concept of speed is often a key component in discussions of the benefits of adopting digital recording practices. Of course, the reality is not so simple, as new digital methods bring with them additional time commitments in the processing and management of data, additional know-how, and financial commitments. However, the critique remains: What is lost when practices move from analogue to digital? Colleen Morgan and Holly Wright have convincingly argued that certain archaeological practices such as hand drawing are necessary pedagogical tools for learning and understanding the complexities of a site. They also highlight the embodied effects of drawing by hand which provide greater possibilities for creative interpretation, whereas relying on digital visualisation techniques constrains creativity because of the limiting affordances of the technology (Morgan and Wright 2018, 146–47). Taylor et al. (2018) have also noted the potential 'digital wedge' that can be hammered into the cycle of interpretation that, in theory, should be occurring as much during excavation as in the laboratory. Instead of a deep engagement with the archaeological record at the trowel's edge, digital recording may force us to breeze past the interpretive step during excavation. Although technologies such as computational photogrammetry are becoming more common as a recording technique, many archaeologists do not see them replacing hand drawing as the main source of spatial recording (Powlesland 2016). There remains a worry that shifting to purely digital techniques, technologies that are often poorly understood, will result in a loss of skill in archaeological work.

This type of 'de-skilling', as Caraher (2016, 435) terms it, is not the only potential issue with a reliance on born-digital recording methods. In her response paper to the *Mobilizing the Past* volume, Morag Kersel asks a salient question of a 'born-digital' archaeological future: 'In going digital, are we establishing an archaeology that excludes individuals who are not technologically inclined?' (2016, 481). There exists a genuine fear that a rapid shift to born-digital recording methods in the field will segment the archaeological community into haves and have nots, or cans and cannots; the haves consist of the projects that are able to afford mobile recording devices or terrestrial laser scanners, or those with the technical knowledge to be able to capture and process digital data. The discrepancy in projects with access to equipment and staff specialists is a complex issue. It is no coincidence that

many of the earliest and most innovative uses of these digital recording techniques occurred at well-funded sites or those with an international profile.
However, there are a few reasons to feel optimistic. First, technological
advancement often requires a dramatic push forward to alter practices on
a large scale. Projects like the Pompeii Archaeological Research Project:
Porta Stabia (Ellis 2016) or Çatalhöyük (Forte 2014) demonstrated that 'big
dig' projects often have the resources to experiment with new technologies,
providing guidelines for smaller projects to follow or adjust to match their own
workflows. Second, digital technologies are becoming more inexpensive and
digital knowledge is becoming more diffuse. Excavations can adopt computational photogrammetry with very limited cost and instructional time. The price
of tablets also continues to decrease, especially if open-source software options
are adopted. A perceived technological distance between projects should not be
the main concern in the move towards born-digital recording practices; there
have always been discrepancies in the resources available to different archaeological projects and unfortunately that is unlikely to change. The most important
aspect of adopting a new field recording method (and any digital technology) is
considering if it will benefit the goals of archaeology and how it may impact the
construction of knowledge that occurs during and after excavation.

The additional concern over a lack of abilities in born-digital recording
remains central. This worry over being 'technologically inclined' or not is
really a concern over the time commitment to learning new skills – not an idle
worry, to be sure. This is once again an example of an issue that has always
plagued archaeologists; how can we develop an expertise in the ever-growing
body of knowledge that is required to practice archaeology? I disagree with the
notion that some archaeologists have an innate ability to learn new digital skills
while others do not. The focus should rather be on whether the new recording
practices discussed in this section are beneficial for the goals of archaeological
work, and if so, what are the ways that we can better integrate the teaching of
these digital skills into pedagogical programs.

3 Visualising Archaeology in New Ways

Section 2 illustrated the rate at which 3D data capture has infiltrated archaeological fieldwork. New types of visualisation have also been adapted for post-
fieldwork use to document artefacts, to provide unique perspectives on cultural
heritage, to create virtual reconstructions of sites, and to immerse users in
heritage experiences. 3D visualisation is not a new practice in archaeological
research. However, in recent years these techniques have become more accessible to the wider archaeological community.

In some cases, digital visualisations are challenging traditional archaeological practices. This is not a new phenomenon in the discipline – new techniques are often viewed with some scepticism initially. When photography developed as a viable documentation tool at the turn of the last century, archaeologists were hesitant to adopt it lest they lose the interpretive power that illustration brought to documentation in favour of the mechanical reproduction of photographs (Garstki 2017). To be clear, a cautious approach to adopting new technology is not inherently a bad thing. In fact, a critical attitude towards new tools avoids the kind of technological fetishism that has already affected archaeology and society as a whole. Through this careful approach, some archaeologists are utilising emerging visualisation techniques to bring new dimensions to archaeological research and ways of seeing.

3.1 Visualisation of Artefacts

Computational photogrammetry has been applied almost as impactfully to artefacts as to archaeological excavations, as discussed in Section 2. Close-range photogrammetry requires limited financial expenditure. The 3D modelling of artefacts using SfM techniques has taken off in the last decade (e.g., Kersten & Lindstaedt 2012; Olson and Caraher 2015; Papadopoulos et al. 2019; Štular and Štuhec 2015; Sapirstein 2018). A simple search on Sketchfab will return hundreds of 3D artefact models created using this technique. At the same time other forms of 3D documentation have also been applied to archaeological objects, including laser scanning (e.g., Amico et al. 2018; Merchán et al. 2011; Pires et al. 2006) and structured or white light scanning (e.g., Counts et al. 2016; Lami et al. 2016; Mara and Bogacz 2016). Each technique used for creating digital 3D artefact representations provides both benefits and drawbacks to documentation. Although techniques like structured light or laser scanning typically provide higher resolution than computational photogrammetry[14] or the NextEngine,[15] the cost is also higher.

As with other forms of 3D documentation in archaeological work, the question must be asked, What are we doing with these models once they have been created? The aesthetic appeal of a digital 3D artefact is clear – the technology is still novel enough that we can marvel at these virtual objects (Video 2). But as these techniques become commonplace in European archaeology, our focus should shift from experimental exercises to research-driven projects. Attempts at using 3D models to supplement traditional text are the first level of purpose-driven approaches to 3D scanning. Counts et al. (2020) and

---

[14] Although this is changing with advances in software and knowledge of proper techniques.

[15] A type of 3D scanner that mixes laser scanning with a proprietary technology.

Video 2 A 3D model of a terracotta mask created using a structured light scanner. The artefact (AAP-AM-5115) is from the Sanctuary at Athienou-*Malloura*, Cyprus. Housed at the Larnaka District Archaeological Museum, Cyprus. Video available at www.cambridge.org/garstki

Štular and Štuhec (2015) both use digital 3D artefacts to act as replacements for illustrations or photographs, documenting limestone and terracotta statuary from Athienou-*Malloura* (Cyprus) and earrings from the Early Medieval site of Kranj (Slovenia), respectively. These approaches demonstrate the many ways in which digital 3D models are superior to 2D representations: they have the ability to be viewed from all angles, one can take accurate measurements on the model (Figure 6), and one can digitally change shading or lighting conditions to highlight certain parts of the model. On the other hand, the use of these models in traditionally formatted publications is still limited. A printed book cannot incorporate a digital 3D model, and most platforms and publishers are only beginning to embed 3D content into digital publications.

But more than acting as aesthetic replacements for 2D representations, digital 3D artefacts can provide useful data to contribute to archaeological research. Geometric morphometrics is an area of study that quantifies analyses based on measured geometric markers on a surface. Although these techniques are currently mostly used on lithic or skeletal elements, they are particularly well suited for analysis on digital 3D objects because the surface geometry is translated into digital form. For example, focused approaches on 3D scans have been demonstrated to be

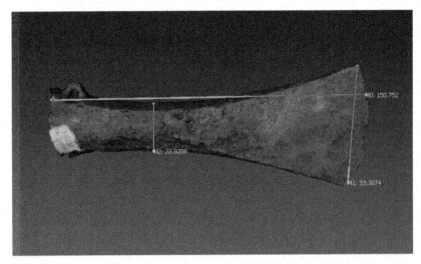

Figure 6 Measurements taken digitally in Meshlab on an Iron Age socketed looped axe from Magdalenska gora, Slovenia. (PM 34–25-40/8721. Peabody Museum of Archaeology and Ethnology)

useful for quantifying Levallois core variability and stability across Europe, Africa, the Near East, and the Indian subcontinent (Lycett and von Cramon-Taubadel 2013). Computer-aided methods can also be applied to digital lithic models to automate the identification of scars and ridges (Richardson et al. 2012).

The reconstruction of fragmented objects has always been essential to archaeological work – artefacts are rarely found whole. The usefulness of using digital 3D models of fragments rests with their accessibility and the fact that they can be studied without damaging them; digital models can be accessed from anywhere rather than trying to physically reconstruct the artefact. For example, pieces of ceramic can be 3D scanned and rendered in a digital environment, and then pieced back together or used to create a digital recreation of the vessel, as in the case of a reconstructed 16th-century ceramic pot from Convent of Santo António de Ferreirim in Lamego, Portugal (Pires et al. 2006). This type of reconstruction can also be applied to sculptural fragments, demonstrated with the Aeneas Group at the Spanish National Museum of Roman Art (Merchán et al. 2011). A potential future direction for fragmentary reconstructions is to use computer-aided matching algorithms to identify joins between different pieces. This approach has been used in efforts to reconstruct the Severan Marble Plan of Rome (Koller 2008) and the frescos from Akrotiri (Brown et al. 2008). A caveat to using these projects as a guide is that they approached reconstruction with largely two dimensions, but in reconstructing most artefacts (pottery, sculptures, figurines, metal objects, etc.) one would have to account for three dimensions of breakage. An additional consideration is whether this approach is actually 'worth it'. To be successful, all objects of the type would have to be scanned, thousands of fragments in some cases – is the final product worth the time commitment?

Considering that an overwhelming amount of artefact modelling is conducted using surface modelling techniques, it is safe to say that most of digital 3D artefact studies are focused on the surface of an artefact. Many 3D viewers provide users with different lighting, shading, or normals[16] visualisation options. Details of an artefact surface can be emphasised by using these different views. Figure 7 shows a comparison of different visualisations of the same digital 3D object, each highlighting different aspects of the original artefact.

Because the surface of artefacts is often a focus of digital analyses, it is unsurprising that other non-3D visualisation techniques like multispectral imaging and reflectance transformation imaging (RTI) have also been applied to archaeological material. RTI is a computational photographic method that records an object's surface with lighting from many angles. The process is based on polynomial texture mapping (PTM), first developed at HP labs two decades ago (Malzbender et al. 2001). The composite digital object, often described as 2.5D, can have light digitally raked across the surface, enhancing surface features (Video 3) (Figure 8). The images can also be rendered differently to highlight different features, such as specular enhancement

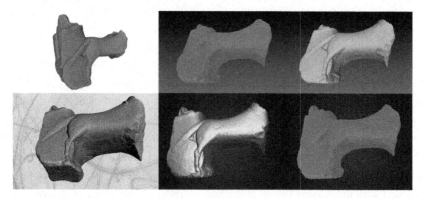

Figure 7 Different rendering of the same fragmentary limestone quadriga from Athienou-*Malloura*, Cyprus (AAP-AM-4260). Housed at the Larnaka District Archaeological Museum, Cyprus. Top: different rendering in Meshlab. Bottom left: rendered in 3DHop. Bottom middle and right: different rendering in Sketchfab.

---

[16] A normal map takes a perpendicular vector of a point surface and artificially colours the x,y,z. This method makes certain angles or ridges more distinct on a model.

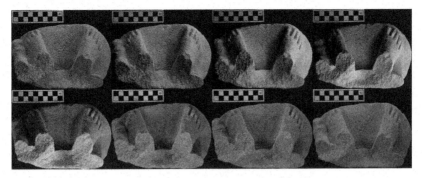

Figure 8 Images showing the RTI raked light across Pan statuette base from Athienou-*Malloura*, Cyprus (AAP-AM-5160). Housed at the Larnaka District Archaeological Museum, Cyprus.

Video 3 An image of the RTI viewer with raking light. The object is a Pan statuette base from Athienou-*Malloura*, Cyprus (AAP-AM-5160). Housed at the Larnaka District Archaeological Museum, Cyprus. Video available at www.cambridge .org/garstki

which highlights surface features with higher reflectance and normals visualisation which produces a false-colour render that highlights surface contours in another way (Figure 9).

RTI is a low-cost option for investigating surface details on archaeological surfaces, as the software to process and view the RTI image is now available for free.[17] The technique has been applied in a variety of research areas, such as numismatics, rock art, epigraphy, and graffiti (Diaz-Guardamino et al. 2015;

---

[17] http://culturalheritageimaging.org/Technologies/RTI/

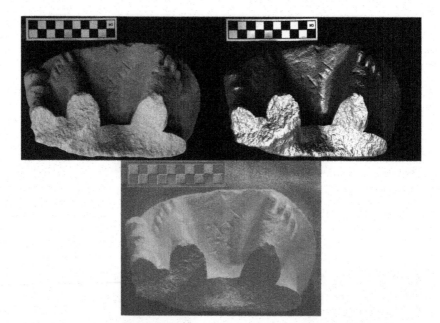

Figure 9 Different rendering options in RTI viewer of Pan statuette base from Athienou-*Malloura*, Cyprus (AAP-AM-5160). Housed at the Larnaka District Archaeological Museum, Cyprus. Top left: standard rending mode. Top right: rendered with specular enhancement. Bottom: rendered with normals visualisation.

Earl et al 2010; Palma et al. 2013; Sammons 2018; Smith et al. 2018). The images can be also used with additional spectral imaging techniques, such as infrared or ultraviolet, and can highlight subsurface features or subtle surface variations (Kotoula and Earl 2015; Kotoula 2016; Papadopoulos et al. 2019). Papadopoulos et al. (2019) have demonstrated some of the most impactful approaches to artefact analysis using RTI. They utilised multiple digital imaging techniques on Greek Neolithic figurines to investigate more multi-sensory and affective approaches to coroplastic studies. Small details like fingerprints and fine brush strokes on figurines exposed not only the productive process of forming the figurine but also a direct connection to the person who formed it: 'A landscape full of traces speaks to the viewer of how human hands shaped, smoothed, worked the clay before firing' (Papadopouloss et al. 2019, 640). The images are not powerful just because of the features that they may help identify but also because of the *affect* that they cause in the viewer, creating a more intimate connection between the modern viewer and the person who formed the object. This approach to 3D (or 2.5D) visualisations demonstrates a real potential for a digitally mediated interaction with the past, utilising imagery to enhance multiple dimensions of archaeological reconstruction.

3.2 Reconstructions and Virtual Reality

The long-held tradition of artistic reconstruction of archaeological contexts actually moved into a digital realm decades ago. Even early in the 1990s Reilly (1991) noted the benefits of creating digital models of archaeological contexts, such as an aide for those visiting Pompeii (134). Architectural reconstructions provide the viewer with something often missing from plan maps or site photographs: a full picture of the structure that once stood there. Forte and Siliotti (1997) demonstrated over two decades ago the potential of computer modelling as an interpretive aide and a number of dedicated institutes have been creating archaeologically based reconstructions for even longer (Pfarr-Harfst 2015). Just as illustrated reconstructions have long been used as aides to help communicate archaeological interpretations to professionals and the public, digital reconstructions have been doing the same. Whether showing diachronic change of a site (Tronchère et al. 2016), helping in conservation (Đuričić 2017), supporting the goals of preventive archaeology (Horňák 2017), or dissemination through video or TV (Alaguero et al. 2015), these types of reconstructions can be powerful visualisations. It is safe to say that at this point digital 3D reconstructions are intimately tied to European archaeology, and the scope and breadth of its role in modern archaeological practice is too great for the scope of this book.

Perhaps the most useful application of digital reconstructions is their use in virtual reality – the ability to move through and interact with the reconstruction. Virtual reality (VR) can be non-immersive when viewed through a computer screen, or immersive, on a head-mounted display or in a large-scale immersive environment (i.e., CAVE). The development of gaming engines in the past two decades (Oikarinen 2016), and an increase in typical hardware capabilities, have allowed VR in archaeology to become more common. Both immersive and non-immersive VR systems provide an enormous benefit to teaching archaeological students, especially as it 'gamifies' the experience of archaeological narratives. Students can experience excavations by being immersed in 3D scenes created using image modelling (e.g., Di Giuseppantonio Di Franco et al. 2012; Forte 2014; Garstki et al. 2019), or experience reconstructed archaeological structures (e.g., Fleury et al. 2015; Rome Reborn).[18] Through VR, we can find possibilities for enhanced storytelling in all aspects of archaeological education: with students, museum visitors, and the general public (see for example Petersson and Larsson 2018). Along these same lines there is also great potential to utilise virtual reconstructions for augmented reality (AR) systems. In AR, normal human experience is supplemented through an additional device, as opposed to the complete replacement of

---

[18] https://www.romereborn.org/content/aboutcontact

experience that occurs with VR. The role AR can have in archaeological contexts has been well demonstrated (Ellenberger 2017; Eve 2017; Tasić 2017b). The recent international VirtualArch[19] project has demonstrated just how flexible and wide-reaching VR and AR can be in archaeological contexts, from an immersive VR reconstruction of the Hallstatt mines to a virtual thriller game that takes place in Buchberg (Unger et al. 2020). Now that most of us have powerful computers in our pockets with high resolution screens and cameras, visitors to archaeological or historical sites can interact with virtual reconstructions in their own landscapes – experiencing the past through their own devices.

Despite the benefits discussed earlier, digital reconstructions of archaeological sites or buildings can suffer from the same problem as previous types of reconstructions – they concretise a 'best guess' at interpreting the archaeological record, leaving little room for nuance or uncertainty. This technology once again demonstrates how many long-standing issues in archaeology are being retread through digital techniques. There was outrage when drawings from Alan Sorrell, the famed artist who created numerous reconstructions of archaeological sites, were used in many British site guides (Lock 2003, 155). And we need look no further than the Neolithic site of Newgrange in Ireland for an example of a physical reconstruction based on the ideas of an archaeologist that has not stood the test of time. Based on M. J. O'Kelly's interpretation of the quartz found at the base of the mound, a façade was reconstructed containing the stones whose authenticity is still hotly debated (Cooney 2006; Eriksen 2004, 2006). Digital reconstructions of archaeological sites have the same failings as physical reconstructions: because the main use of reconstruction is to communicate interpretations to a non-professional public, their authenticity carries significant weight, based upon the perceived claims to authority. There are, unfortunately, limited ways to build uncertainty into the digital reconstructions themselves. This accentuates the need to combine reconstructions with text or other interactive media that situate this single interpretation into a larger archaeological narrative.

3.3 Publication of 3D Data

Despite the rapid creation of 3D archaeological data, challenges to the publication and easy distribution of these data continue. As outlined in this and Section 2, massive amounts of 3D data are created in modern European archaeology. As the discipline continues to try and outline best practices for the long-term management and use of data in general, there is also a concerted effort to do so for 3D digital data. There have been a few recent, innovative books that have advanced the ways that 3D content can be disseminated via more traditional publication

---

[19] https://www.interreg-central.eu/Content.Node/VirtualArch.html

strategies, but without losing the functionality of 3D models. For example, Štular and Štuhec's (2015) *3D Archaeology: Early Medieval Earrings from Kranj* maintained the structure of a traditional catalogue of artefacts but presented the material in digital form (through iBooks) and embedded 3D models of the featured earrings. This publication brought a new level of accessibility to the digital 3D content, placing it alongside the typical archaeological textual content in a form that could be used by someone unfamiliar with the technology. *A Mid-Republican House from Gabii* (Opitz et al. 2016) is another example of an extremely ambitious publication that attempted to fully integrate archaeological narrative, 'raw' data archiving, and 3D media. The authors utilised a bespoke system developed in conjunction with the publisher to visualise and interact with all levels of archaeological content, at times simultaneously. They also approached their narrative presentation with an eye towards accessibility, usability, and an appeal to a wider readership (Opitz 2018 outlines the thought processes that went into many of the publication choices). Due to the many ways in which this publication challenged traditional excavation monograph models (embedded 3D content, viewing platform, narrative form, data accessibility), it will surely act as a future model for ways to push archaeological publication forward, finding ways to integrate digital 3D data more directly with traditional monographs.

However, despite some important forays into the publication of 3D content in traditional mediums, dissemination of these data has remained largely through web-based platforms (see Champion and Rahaman 2020 for recent overview). Sketchfab remains the most popular platform for publishing and sharing 3D content of archaeological sites or material. Sketchfab is a for-profit platform that uses WebGL[20] technology as the basis for its 3D viewer. Originally developed for gaming models, its ease of use was quickly recognised by archaeologists to display their 3D content. There are many reasons why this platform is so popular: models can be uploaded at no cost (but with restrictions), the 3D viewer can be embedded in various websites including social media like Facebook and Twitter, and annotations can highlight different features of the model for the viewer. A number of prominent European museums are displaying 3D models of their collections through Sketchfab. The Rmn-Grand Palais Sketchfab[21] account contains 734 models at the time of writing and the British Museum[22] maintains a robust collection on Sketchfab with 255 models (Figure 10). Additional museums with smaller collections of 3D models on display include Kunsthistorisches Museum, Wien,[23] Fitzwilliam Museum,[24] and Kulturhistorik Museum, Universitetet I Oslo.[25]

---

[20] A common JavaScript API that renders interactive 2D or 3D content.
[21] https://sketchfab.com/francecollections   [22] https://sketchfab.com/britishmuseum
[23] https://sketchfab.com/KunsthistorischesMuseumWien
[24] https://sketchfab.com/fitzwilliammuseum   [25] https://sketchfab.com/khm

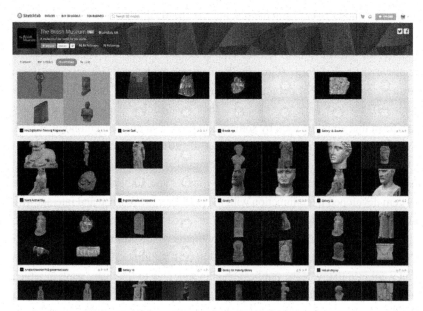

Figure 10 Sketchfab page of the British Museum.

Yet as useful as this platform is for the easy dissemination of 3D archaeological models, its structure creates some issues when dealing with heritage data. First, there is a pay structure that restricts the number of uploads, restricts the number of private versus public models, and restricts the number of non-downloadable models that can be uploaded in a given month. These restrictions are mitigated by making one's models available for download or purchase. Thus, as a for-profit company, their model is to monetise the use of this platform through subscription fees and purchasing of models. In terms of best practices of data sustainability, this platform is not an archive: the data do not preserve if you discontinue services or if the company fails or is sold. Although ease of use and accessibility of data are appealing for archaeologists, there should also be supplements for this type of dissemination that take into account the sustainability and permanence of the information.

Another option for 3D web visualisation of archaeological data is 3DHOP[26] (3D Heritage Online Presenter), developed by the Visual Computing Lab of ISTI-CNR (Potenziani et al. 2015). 3DHOP is an open-source software package for presenting 3D models, specifically developed for the cultural heritage field. This tool is meant to be used by institutions creating their own platform for 3D heritage models. Through Ariadne's Visual Media Service,[27] one can publish and present 3D models using the 3DHOP visualiser and share these URLs with

---

[26] http://3dhop.net/index.php   [27] http://visual.ariadne-infrastructure.eu/

others (archaeological data that are uploaded are kept private and only accessed by linking directly to the object). It should be noted that just like Sketchfab, the Visual Media Service is not an archive and data should be stored elsewhere for long-term management.

A few platforms have begun to use 3DHOP to visualise 3D content within broader structures of data preservation. The Archaeology Data Service (ADS), UK, began a project to investigate the use of 3DHOP as a web-based 3D environment housed in the ADS[28] (Galeazzi et al. 2016). Additionally, Open Context has begun using 3DHOP to visualise 3D data published and archived through their services. Their initial foray into visualising 3D content in this way was with artefact models created as part of the Athienou Archaeological Project's (Cyprus) *Visualizing Votive Practice: Exploring Limestone and Terracotta Sculpture from Athienou-Malloura through 3D Models.* The project's central focus is a digital artefact catalogue with 3D models of 50 limestone and terracotta sculptural fragments embedded in the text (Counts et al. 2020). In addition to the digital monograph, each artefact entry is mirrored in a record on Open Context,[29] which includes a 3D model of the artefact. This type of publication strategy for 3D content makes use of varied platforms and infrastructures, distributing the onus of archiving and media display. A similar approach was established for the 3D ICONS[30] project, funded through the European Commission's ICT Policy Support Programme, whose aim was to develop a workflow for 3D data capture, processing, and publication of archaeological material. As with the other examples discussed earlier, this project worked through an existing infrastructure, Europeana, for the publication of digital 3D content. An important product of 3D ICONS was the structuring and establishment of a comprehensive metadata and paradata scheme that will increase the (re)usability of the 3D models as digital resources (D'Andrea and Fernie 2013).

3.4 Authenticity, Authority, and Ownership

Despite the overwhelming adoption of 3D scanning and modelling of archaeological artefacts, the reception of their use has been far from consistent. The reality is that these technologies have taken off so rapidly in archaeology that there has been uncritical use of the digital products of the 3D scanning process. I have previously highlighted the need for all those producing and using digital 3D artefact representations to be aware of the processes by which they are created (Garstki 2017; 2018). This technology suffers from a similar problem

---

[28] https://archaeologydataservice.ac.uk/research/3DViewer.xhtml
[29] https://opencontext.org/projects/116-visualizing-votive-practice-exploring-limestone-and-te
[30] http://3dicons.ceti.gr/index.php

discussed in Section 2, a back-boxing of the techniques, which leads to an assumption of objective creation not unlike early photography (Bourdieu 1996; Bohrer 2011). Photography was initially viewed as a form of mechanical reproduction (sensu Benjamin 1968), an objective form of documentation that removed any creativity from the process of representation. However, photography requires myriad choices in photographic settings that are controlled by the photographer. This is also the case for the creation of 3D objects – for example, the different types of technologies used to create 3D models outlined earlier all provide different outcomes, even when modelling the same artefact. Many choices are made and actions taken during the production of a 3D model, representing the human side of this 'mechanical reproduction'. To account for these choices, many archaeologists are maintaining robust records of the model paradata (or process metadata), although there remains no standard for these data specific to archaeological models.

An accompanying feature of the widespread use of 3D technology in archaeology is authority. Archaeologists and cultural heritage professionals have always occupied a place of power and authority over heritage materials. Di Giuseppantonio Di Franco et al. note that 'archaeologists are the first people to experience the object during its discovery. After studying the object and giving their personal/subjective interpretation, they give back to the public an "authentic" piece of their cultural past' (2018b, 3). They suggest that through an increased use of 3D digital replicas (their phrase), the possibilities are opened for participation of 'non-expert' users and producers in the narratives surrounding cultural heritage (Di Giuseppantonio Di Franco et al. 2018b, 4). However, despite some examples of community generated 3D heritage content,[31] the majority of digital 3D artefact representations are created by those in archaeology or the heritage sector. As a result, I argue that a great deal of authority still lies with the 'experts' who are creating the models; authority because of the technological skill they appear to hold and the artefacts they choose to 3D scan (Garstki 2018). By choosing to scan only certain pieces, often the 'best' or most museum-worthy, the producer has the authority to control which archaeological content reaches an audience. Perhaps transparency in 3D production will help to mitigate some of this authority but it may be an unfortunate by-product of any aspect of the discipline. Standards for producing and sharing digital content do exist, such as the London Charter (Hermon and Niccolucci 2018) or CARERE metadata scheme (D'Andrea and Fernie 2013), but there is nothing forcing someone to follow these guidelines.

Authority is attributed to archaeologists or cultural heritage professionals in part due to the presumption that they are presenting an 'authentic' view of the

---

[31] The ACCORD (Archaeological Community Co-Production of Research Resources) project, for example (Jones et al. 2018), elaborated on in Section 5. See also the Re-reading the British Memorial Project (OuRTI) (Beale and Beale 2015).

past. Physical casts, replicas, or epigraphic squeezes are old forms of reproduction in archaeology that developed prior to the professionalisation of the discipline (Beard 1994; Joy and Elliot 2018; Rabinowitz 2015). They were often a way for museums to display objects without endangering the original artefacts or to facilitate loans to other museums. Producing digital representations of artefacts and other pieces of cultural heritage is accompanied by an expectation that the virtual artefact is authentic to the original object, and to date, the way authenticity of digital 3D artefacts is perceived is extremely varied (see Di Giuseppantonio Di Franco et al. 2018a for different perspectives). At times accuracy is confused with authenticity, but they need not be interchangeable. If they were indeed the same we'd have to ask the question, What level of accuracy is required for authenticity to be achieved: a micron accuracy on the surface, the same RGB colour value on the phototexture? But pure quantification of authenticity ignores the affective nature of 3D digital representations and sidelines human experience. Instead, authenticity has been argued to emerge through the productive process of creating a 3D model, meaningful to those who were involved in the production (Jeffrey 2015; 2018; Jones 2010; Jones and Yarrow 2013). It has also been suggested that authenticity is a feature unable to transfer from physical artefact to digital representation due to the perception of 'pastness' of an object that is tied to its physical being (Garstki 2017). What these views have in common, although they may seem to be opposed to one another, is that it is the *experience* of a digital object that invites calls of authentic or inauthentic rather than a quantified measurement. Despite existing in a digital realm, the experience is human.

However, the digital realm is precisely why 3D digital representations suffer from their mono-sensorial nature – they privilege visuality over any other sensory experiences (Eve 2018; Papadopoulos et al. 2019). One way to counter this issue is to utilise digital haptic interfaces that allow a person to hold or handle an artefact in a virtual space, but this approach is still limited. A more accessible method for providing digital artefacts with additional sensory information is to 3D print them. 3D prints of digital models add another dimension to the visual experience of a 3D digital representation of an artefact. These physical models can be used for direct interaction or teaching (Di Giuseppantonio Di Franco et al. 2016), or to replace museum pieces on display (Amico et al. 2018). A physical print of an artefact reintroduces a haptic interaction with artefacts and makes this type of experience accessible to more than professional archaeologists who are typically the only ones to ever handle an artefact. Although standard 3D printing materials fail to capture the texture of most artefacts, this technology continues to improve and it is likely that the production of physical replicas will only increase.

As 3D printing technology is refined and as 3D scanning of artefacts becomes more common in archaeology, a major dilemma that we will face surrounds the idea of ownership of digital objects. Just as in other areas of the heritage sector, digital artefacts have the potential to act as nexuses of different stakeholders, often with different perceptions of ethical heritage and ownership rights. The 3D printing and reconstruction of the Triumphal Arch from Palmyra demonstrated the potential for complex national and international politics to play out with digital artefacts (Khunti 2018). As a response to the destruction of the Roman period site in Palmyra, Syria, by ISIS terrorists who had also murdered hundreds of local people, the Institute of Digital Archaeology (IDA) decided to 3D print a reconstruction of one of the most famous structures at the site, the Arch of Triumph. This large-scale 3D print was displayed in London, New York, and Dubai to much pomp and circumstance. Unfortunately, the events surrounding the unveiling of the Arch did not focus attention on or help the Syrian people impacted most by the destruction of Palmyra. Roshni Khunti noted that 'the executive director of the IDA, as well as the Mayors of London and New York, presented the reconstructed arch as a response to the suffering in Syria, which detracts from the fact that none of them actually pledged to actively improve the lives of the people in conflict' (2018, 3). By limiting who can use digital objects we risk disenfranchising the most important stakeholders of the heritage.

Yet the question of who can use this digital content of cultural heritage is not yet well established. In most cases archaeological objects cannot be copyrighted, as they exist in the public domain. However, museums or other institutions retain physical ownership of the objects even if they do not hold copyright of the artefact – generally in the EU, ownership does not mean copyright. Where it becomes tricky is when 3D digital representations are created of those artefacts. A long-standing battle over the 3D scans of the Bust of Nefertiti held by the Neues Museum in Berlin came to a digital end recently with the release of an official 3D scan of the bust. This followed a standoff with the Stiftung Preußischer Kulturbesitz (Prussian Cultural Heritage Foundation) who initially cited loss of financial gain as the reason for not releasing the scans (Bishara 2019). Interestingly, the museum placed a Creative Commons license on the scan that did not allow it to be used for commercial purposes which only complicates the debate of whether a 3D model of an object in the public domain can be copyrighted. A debate similarly occurred when the UK National Portrait Gallery in London had an issue with a student downloading images from the Gallery and posting them on Wikimedia Commons, a case that never reached the courts (Petri 2014). In the United States, the case *Bridgeman Art Library v. Corel Corp.* from 1999 set the precedent that digital photographic images of uncopyrightable objects (e.g., art) cannot be claimed under intellectual property rights (Blackwell and Blackwell 2013). Though not a European case, this may indicate how European courts would trend. These cases get to the heart of the conflict of ownership and digital representations – who should 'own' the digital data that are produced from an artefact, the producer (often an archaeologist) or the institution that possesses the original? Far from being a legal, semantic argument, this question of ownership will have repercussions for the ways 3D digital representations of artefacts can and will be used in the future and will frame their role in ethical socio-political dialogues. However, what is most important to remember in these battles over ownership and copyright of digital 3D models is that they do not negate the colonial seizure and continued holding of cultural heritage from their place of origin, regardless of how good the 3D scan is.

4 Data Archiving, Dissemination, and Publication

The amount of digital data collected during archaeological excavations and analyses is ever-increasing. These data include primary excavation data either recorded digitally or transferred from analogue records; visual data in the form of digital excavation photos, digitised plan and section maps; GIS infrastructures; digital artefact photos; collections and specialist data recording. This does not even include the many projects incorporating 3D excavation models, 3D artefact models, or remote sensing techniques including LiDAR prospection and various geophysical investigations. Finally, we are witnessing massive digitisation projects which are moving analogue records from years past into digital formats. Multiply this by the thousands of archaeological projects conducted in Europe and archaeology is clearly in the midst of a 'data deluge', as Andrew Bevan famously suggested (2015). Archaeologists throughout Europe must be aware not only of the current challenges posed by this data overload but also understand the future ramifications of these massive data accumulations.

The exponential growth of data being created can no longer be handled using traditional modes of management, storage, or dissemination. In the inaugural edition of *Internet Archaeology* 25 years ago, Alan Vince wrote about the changing forms of data dissemination and how digital technologies (specifically the Internet) could be the way forward.

> The earliest solution was to disseminate data in printed form, either as photocopied 'grey literature' or through the use of microfiche. This was followed by attempts to make electronic data a part of site archives. This attempt has not had any noticeable success, mainly because of the difficulties in curating electronic data. The third method proposed was to disseminate electronic archives on disk or CD-ROM. This is at the time of writing the preferred option of most archaeologists in the UK. However, as one might expect from the editorial of an electronic journal on the World Wide Web, I believe there is a better way. (Vince 1996)

Indeed, CD-ROM is no longer a viable means for storing or disseminating archaeological data for many reasons, not least of which is that most new computers (specifically laptops) no longer have a CD-ROM drive. But, significantly, archaeologists are also realising that much of the potential of archaeological data rests in the possibilities for reuse and consolidation with other, related data. To realise this potential, archaeologists must acknowledge the necessity of thinking about the future when it comes to the management of data. Long-term storage, dissemination, publication, and interoperability are all aspects of a broader data management strategy, and all have different and unique challenges to overcome. The development of best practices and standards for preserving and sharing archaeological data in Europe has made significant strides in recent years. As a result, we are beginning to see the benefits to the discipline and to digital heritage management more broadly.

Section 4 focuses on what happens after archaeologists produce their data, including the ways that digital technologies have provided new opportunities for the discipline to expand the potential of those data and create platforms to engage more deeply with them. As the open access mentality infiltrates all levels of archaeological practice, remaining challenges to these approaches include quantity of data, traditional publishing infrastructures and policies, and existing technological limitations. However, innovations over the last decade-plus have created a strong foundation on which to build for the future.

4.1 Digital Archiving

The basic concept of data archiving may seem like a natural progression from data creation, one that has rested at the centre of archaeological practice for the last century. However, placing written documents in a filing cabinet or on a shelf is no longer a practical or sustainable strategy for preserving the massive amounts of information created as part of the archaeological process. Similarly, creating digital data and storing it on a personal hard drive or cloud server does not preserve the information for any longer than the limited run of a project or at most an archaeologist's career. Stuart Jeffrey (2012) outlined how a 'digital dark age' occurred as digital technology improved, data corrupted, and hardware and software became obsolete. To avoid another digital dark age, archaeology has begun to establish nationally controlled or independent non-profit repositories for data that also act as digital archives, with the explicit goal of outlasting changes to technological systems.

The first of these archives to preserve and make archaeological data accessible was the Archaeology Data Service (ADS)[32] which began in 1996 as

---

[32] https://archaeologydataservice.ac.uk/

a collaboration between a number of universities in the UK; it was part of the Arts and Humanities Data Service for a decade before it became an independent entity. The ADS curates and preserves digital archaeological data and provides free access to many pieces of heritage data including metadata records, unpublished reports, and in some cases full databases.

Another well-established digital archive that includes archaeological data in its mission is the Data Archive and Networked Services (DANS)[33] which is an institute of the Royal Netherlands Academy of Arts and Sciences and the Netherlands Organisation for Scientific Research. A number of systems are managed within DANS, including services for short-term data management, long-term archiving, and the national gateway for research information. The archaeological collection comprises the e-Depot Nederlandse Archeologie which includes datasets and reports by Dutch archaeologists and projects based in the Netherlands. DANS maintains an open access/data approach to its archived information but with restricted access when necessary. Other national repositories include the Mappa Open Data (MOD)[34] project in Italy, the Swedish National Data Service (SND)[35] in Sweden, and Arachne[36] in Germany. MOD includes data and reports mainly from archaeology and related disciplines in Italy. Arachne is the central object database of the German Archaeological Institute (DAI) and the Archaeological Institute of the University of Cologne, and acts as a free research tool for digital data (often media) of the DAI's collections. Its structure makes use of principles of the semantic web by linking other aspects of the DAI infrastructure (DAI.welt; DAI.bibliography; DAI.gazetter).

Two archives and repositories in the US, Open Context and the Digital Archaeological Record (tDAR),[37] represent similar goals to these open data models of data archiving and include data from European archaeological contexts. tDAR is an international digital repository for archaeological data, maintained by Digital Antiquity. Data archived through this source are largely freely accessible. Open Context[38] is a data publisher and repository, maintained by the Alexandria Archive Institute. Although Open Context does archive data through the University of California library system, it approaches data deposition and accessibility differently than previously mentioned archives. Because they view themselves as 'data publishers' as much as an archive, Open Context curates and peer reviews data deposited with the service. Both repositories follow Creative Commons licenses that provide differing levels of open access to the archived data.

The ADS, tDAR, and Open Context all currently employ a depositor-charging policy to fund the curation and preservation of the data archived

---

[33] https://dans.knaw.nl/en   [34] http://mappaproject.arch.unipi.it/mod/Index.php
[35] https://snd.gu.se/sv   [36] https://arachne.dainst.org/info/about
[37] https://www.tdar.org/about/   [38] https://opencontext.org/about/

through their system. This fee is necessary to ensure the organisations are able to support the maintenance of these large datasets. Though necessary, it also remains a limitation to some archaeologists who may not have access to additional funds for this type of data management. In cases where archaeological projects are not supported by larger funding bodies, the onus of best data archiving practices then rests with the individual. The financial limitations thus act as a barrier to consistent data archiving across Europe, where well-funded projects are able to sustainably archive their information.

4.2 Interoperability

Another major challenge arising in Europe is the lack of consistency in archiving standards across political boundaries, as well as lack of resources available for proper archiving practices. Only a few countries have institutionally run archives for archaeological data, while others rely on smaller-scale museum or library repositories. This lack of international standards endangers the longevity of the data and the opportunities for their use in the future. The enormous amount of digital data created only remains sustainably useful if there are ways to access and use them. The recent COST ACTION SEADDA[39] is aimed at addressing many of the problems outlined in Section 4. 'Saving European Archaeology from the Digital Dark Age' is an international project funded through the EU that will provide guidelines for best practices in preservation, dissemination, and reuse of archaeological data across national borders. This collaboration will hopefully mitigate some of the discrepancies across European countries with regard to the futures of archaeological data and knowledge production.

The goal of endeavours like SEADDA is to create interoperable archaeological datasets. Interoperability is a characteristic in computing that establishes connections between systems, platforms, and content that allows information to be exchanged and utilised by other sources. In the context of European archaeology this principle has manifested itself in the way that web-based data repositories, archives, or gazetteers structure their archaeological data so that they can link to connected data from other sources. The reasons for creating interoperable data are as much future-looking as they are for immediate use. To maximise the potential for data, we must consider them in their full contexts, including the ways they relate to other available data. By establishing practices and standards that structure the way our data communicate with each other, we are creating a foundation for more powerful analyses to be conducted in the future that utilise the massive web of archaeological data we will have created. We also provide ourselves with the best opportunities for reusing the data we create if they are structured in mutually intelligible ways.

---

[39] https://www.seadda.eu/

We can look to a few of the large digital research infrastructures in Europe that demonstrate the compelling potential for these frameworks for archaeology. These infrastructures act as nodes to connect datasets distributed across the continent. One benefit of this strategy is that it distributes the onus of archiving and curation rather than relying on a single institution for curating all European archaeological data; these infrastructures make the data accessible in a single place. Although not limited to archaeology, Europeana[40] provides access to more than fifty million digitised cultural heritage objects and is the largest e-infrastructure of European cultural material. This massive network makes use of the resources from museums, archives, educational institutions, and libraries, including digitised text, photos of artefacts, and 3D content. In a similar vein, the largest archaeological digital infrastructure is ARIADNE[41], which currently brings together over two million datasets of European archaeology. ARIADNE (now ARIADNEplus, an extension of the original project) had the goal of developing an archaeology-specific infrastructure for Europe that can support and integrate data archived in stable repositories, such as DAI, DANS, and SND (Aloia 2017; Richards and Niccolucci 2019). The data are maintained by their host institutions but ARIADNE uses their metadata to make them findable and accessible. In addition to being an extensive resource to access datasets across Europe through the ARIADNE portal, the next phase of the programme includes a number of research-focused web services that are aimed at data analyses, visualisation, and integration.

Additionally, digital gazetteers and other stable platforms are being used as important complementary datasets to the archaeological data deposited in archives and connected through shared metadata schema and other standards. Pleiades,[42] a community-built gazetteer of ancient places, provides a stable resource to link to for ancient locations around the Mediterranean[43], for example. Another similar resource is Perio.do,[44] a chronological gazetter that 'documents specific published assertions about periods, including their names, their extent in space and time, and when, where, and by whom these assertions were made' (Shaw et al. 2018). The significant benefit of this gazetteer is to mitigate 'talking past each other' when using period descriptors to reference a specific time span at a single location. These resources thus aid in further developing a suite of curated and maintained data that can be linked together to further the potential of those data.

The current focus in European archaeology is to achieve the 'next level' of interoperability for datasets via the concept of Linked Open Data, a group of

---

[40] https://www.europeana.eu/en   [41] https://ariadne-infrastructure.eu/

[42] https://pleiades.stoa.org/

[43] It is expanding to include more temporal and spatial coverage across Europe and the Near East.

[44] http://perio.do/en/

guidelines with the goal of establishing best practices for disseminating digital things (Elliot et al. 2014). As Tim Berners-Lee (2006), best known as the inventor of the World Wide Web, put it, 'the Semantic Web is not just about putting data on the web. It is about making links, so that a person or machine can explore the web of data. With linked data, when you have some of it, you can find other, related, data'. The principles of Linked Data underlie much of what archaeologists are trying to do in Europe with their data moving forward. The CIDOC CRM[45] is now the standard schema for how to structure and define cultural heritage data and their relationships. These shared standards for data organisation allow for easy cross-platform interoperability, from Open Context to Pleiades, for example (Kansa 2014). Large digital infrastructures like ARIADNE compile datasets using a standard metadata schema. For example, you can search by sites in a geographic region of Europe and your searches return metadata on a single site that may include type of site, date, publisher (institution from which the data came), allowing access to the data through the institutional repository (depending on the scope of the data license). However, to date it has been difficult to create wide semantic standards across institutions and countries to become a truly semantically linked web of European archaeo- logical data (Geser 2016, see Huggett 2012 for an important discussion on standards in archaeology). And though in an ideal future each data point (a pottery sherd, iron bracelet, excavation trench) would have its own unique, stable URI to be linked to, this is nowhere close to a reality for the majority of archaeological data (but see ISAW Papers 7[46] 'Current Practice in Linked Open Data for the Ancient World' (2014) for important strides made in Classical Archaeology).

4.3 Publication

We have come to a potential turning point in academic publishing with the increasing ubiquity of computing technology in not just in European archae- ology but science and humanities research writ large. For the last century publishing in European archaeology has existed mainly in traditional forms such as monographs, excavation reports, and edited volumes by established publishers and peer-reviewed academic journals. However, with a disciplinary shift in the expectation of information availability, and the expansion of techno- logical capabilities of web platforms and computing power, we may be witness- ing a shift in publication models.

The transition towards a more open and innovative publication model is not a particularly new concept in European archaeology, to be sure. In the first issue of

---

[45] http://www.cidoc-crm.org/   [46] http://dlib.nyu.edu/awdl/isaw/isaw-papers/7/

Internet Archaeology (1996), Alan Vince noted that, ' ... our professional publications are widely acknowledged to be daunting and dull, even to other professionals. The reason, in my opinion, is that we are drowning in our own data'. Indeed, the creation of traditional archaeological publications suffers from either being too 'data heavy' and losing the attention of scholars or being too synthetic, obscuring the data that informed the interpretations. When it was first published in 1996, *Internet Archaeology* provided a publication platform that adheres to many of the principles of archaeological publication that are still in demand today: non-profit and the inclusion of dynamic media. Although now open access, this is a more recent development for *Internet Archaeology*. *Archeologia e Calcolatore*, on the other hand, has been open access since its inception thirty years ago.

A number of open access journals now exist to support this broader movement in archaeology. However, many of the top journals maintain a tiered system of open access, with green open access being on one level and full (gold)[47] open access on another, requiring subvention funds from the author. Similarly, the few publishers who will publish books in an open access format typically require subvention funds. The reason for these additional supporting funds is logical – if there is no money coming in from print sales, there is no money to support the people who do the work of publishing. Because of this need for revenue, hybrid forms of publication are becoming more common, where a digital open access version is produced as well as a paid print copy. Unfortunately, the only way that publishers will move to a completely open access publication model is if state or international funding is available, which is unlikely in the current political climate.

Further integrating archaeological datasets with peer-reviewed publication should continue to be a goal of modern publishing. Projects published within the LEAP[48] initiative through *Internet Archaeology* demonstrated the significant benefit of making source data accessible to readers for reuse or reproduction of analyses. Connecting data directly to text publication is also a necessity for dynamic media, such as 3D content. Although embedding these media in downloadable publications is not typically possible due to file size limitations, some projects (see Section 3.3) are utilising external archives to link directly to publications. It is therefore important that non-profit, heritage-specific platforms are beginning to not only accept 3D datasets but to also provide accessible visualisers. One major roadblock to the reuse of 3D data is the technical limitations of potential users. By providing an accessible platform through

---

[47] Green open access means an author can post a post-review, pre-formatted publication for free; gold open access means the final publication can be made available for free.

[48] https://intarch.ac.uk/leap/

which to view and access these data, while also seamlessly connecting them to traditional publications, I anticipate a higher likelihood of their reuse.

4.4 Open Archaeology

The trends outlined in this section each share a conceptual shift in ownership to one of openness. Moving to a fully open archaeology that includes data archives and open access publication requires us to address some issues and concerns. Significant coordination across national and disciplinary boundaries is needed to maintain standards of data collection, metadata, and archiving practices. EU-wide infrastructures are well on the way to securing such standards, but the reality remains that only a small fraction of archaeological data are connected through these systems.

European archaeologists are beginning to look outside the discipline for standardised principles to structure these digital data. One recent example of this is the FAIR data principles[49] (Figure 11). Developed by an interdisciplinary group of international scholars, these principles represent a simplified framework for creating, maintaining, and reusing data (Wilkinson et al. 2016). These principles have been explicitly and implicitly applied to archaeological data, expanding the sustainability of digital data in archaeological practice.

The 'A' (Accessibility) has become an important aspect of European archaeology specifically, and science throughout the world more broadly. As discussed earlier, open access includes providing access to the pieces that make up archaeological knowledge: data, methods, interpretation (Lake 2012). It is also about transparency regarding how archaeology is practiced and making information accessible, free of cost and copyright, to those who have a stake in its use. This push towards open access and open data in archaeology has been possible because of the rise of the Internet. Web platforms and archiving services can operate at much lower costs, increasing the ease of accessibility,

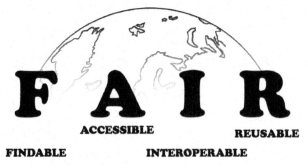

Figure 11 The FAIR data principles.

---

[49] https://www.go-fair.org/fair-principles/

all while creating a space for free access to everything from raw data to published text. This approach provides two options often absent in traditional archaeology: reproducibility and reinterpretation. Open data in particular allows one to revisit the processes by which an archaeologist arrived at their conclusions, bringing different experiences and viewpoints to the derivative data (Beck and Neylon 2012). In addition to the data, providing open code (for the analyses run on the data) and using open-source software leads to a more accessible archaeology, one characterised by the reuse of data (Edwards and Wilson 2015).

The unfortunate barrier to making the ideals of reusability a reality is that most open data sources are not yet ready for widespread reuse. Many research infra-structures and data repositories are difficult to navigate, especially for those less familiar with these kinds of web platforms. Platform-usability will need to be a central focus moving forward if we want data to be used to their full potential. The issue of standardisation also requires some attention. Standardisation neces-sitates equal access to technology and modes of recording, as well as agreed-upon knowledge-making practices. The lack of standardisation, from region to region or from project to project, will remain a concern in how open data connect to each other. Furthermore, standards pose a difficult epistemological problem when considering how the archaeological record is represented (Huggett 2012). The metadata that describe these datasets are often reductive, with limited potential for reusing multiple datasets together. At the moment, little more can be done with these metadata other than querying geographical or temporal information, or standard types (e.g., types of sites or artefacts).

The open access movement seeks to produce changes to policies that have traditionally governed what information must be made available and who is able to access it (Kansa 2012). This approach is, of course, influenced by contemporary socio-political contexts and is subject to specific regional and cultural understandings of how archaeology should be used in modern mean-ing-making. Although open data has the potential to allow access to archaeo-logical stakeholders, it remains important to approach the implementation of open practices in archaeology in a context-by-context basis to avoid reinfor-cing unequal power dynamics. Considerable thought needs to go into ensur-ing that openly available information does no harm to cultural heritage or associated stakeholder communities. Geospatial information is often made opaque in open repositories, in an effort to avoid looting or destruction of sites. Of course, if the precise locations of sites are obscured, this creates a problem for utilising the full potential of archaeological data to look at landscape or regional patterning through linked datasets. This is where a commitment to openness of archaeology conflicts with reality. Archaeologists must also consider how data can be used against stakeholder

Figure 12 The CARE data principles.

groups, for example, in identity claims or land disputes. The broad open science movement typically does not include issues of indigenous peoples' rights and interests. The CARE Principles[50] for Indigenous Data Governance has recently been outlined to accompany the FAIR principles discussed earlier (Figure 12). The CARE principles highlight the need for digital ecosystems to be designed for the collective benefit of indigenous peoples and/or local stakeholders so that control of data rests with the groups most closely connected to it, allowing the data to be shared responsibly.

Open data systems and repositories clearly have the potential to benefit archaeological research throughout Europe. But these concerns remind us that archaeological data are not and should not be disconnected from people, past or present. Archaeological data are meaningful in part due to how they are mobilised by modern people. This is precisely why archaeology has always been a public discipline.

5 Engaging the Public and Inclusive Archaeology

The ability to engage productively with the public has been a feature of European archaeology for most of its history. Half a century ago Sir Mortimer Wheeler suggested that, 'it is the duty of the archaeologist, as of the scientist, to reach and impress the public, and to mould his words in the common clay of its forthright understanding' (1954, 196). If we are to follow Wheeler's suggestion regarding this fundamental duty of archaeologists, *all* archaeology should be viewed as public archaeology, as work performed with and for the non-archaeological public. The degree to which this credo is practiced may certainly be debated, yet what is clear is that digital platforms have already begun to create a more inclusive archaeology in Europe, expanding the role of a myriad of stakeholders, and extending the impact of archaeological work beyond the academy.

---

[50] https://www.gida-global.org/care

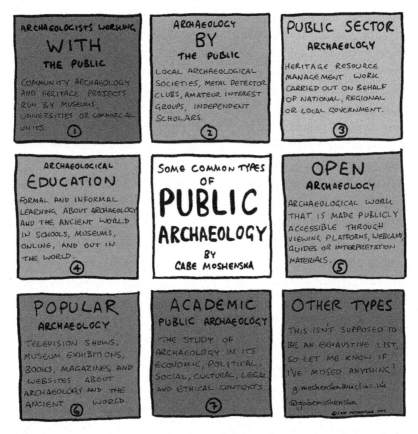

Figure 13 Diagram of some common types of public archaeology. (Created by Gabriel Moshenska)

Gabriel Moshenska's diagram (Figure 13) provides a useful guide to thinking through the variety of components that may be considered under the category of public archaeology. Each of these common types have been touched in some way by the rise of digital technologies. Archaeologists, particularly in Britain, have utilised 3D scanning and visualisation techniques for community co-production as a way to work *with* the public, as in Moshenska's diagram. The Micropasts[51] project, for example, is focused on archaeology conducted *by* the public. Museums and tourist sites have made use of virtual and augmented reality to further *educate* the public on archaeology through popular media, while at the same time social media platforms have provided a digital space for educational outreach and (often frustrating) dialogue. The adoption of open data trends in European archaeology (see Section 4) has created publicly accessible

---

[51] https://crowdsourced.micropasts.org/

archaeological information, providing access to the archaeological process. Finally, the use of digital techniques and platforms for public engagement has brought to the fore important discussions of how archaeology is practiced as a digital discipline; it is situated within social, economic, and ethical realms that impact both how archaeology is done in Europe as well as how it directly impacts stakeholder communities. The opening of digital communities brings with it numerous ethical concerns that have only recently been considered (Richardson 2018). As such, any discussion of a digital public archaeology must also include the living stakeholders who are affected by research using these platforms. Section 6 will address these different components of a digital public archaeology and the ways in which the digital world has impacted these practices.

5.1 Public Archaeology

Museums have traditionally served as the primary mediators between archaeologists and the public. Narratives are designed and conveyed to visitors through these institutions, many of whom rely on these experiences to inform their understanding of the past. As a result, these institutions are incredibly important for public education. Digital tools are transforming the types of interactions taking place in museums, and their adoption can be seen as 'a globalizing instrument with the power of making stories new and different, and in this sense, digitisation is a world-changing process' (Petersson and Larsson 2018, 70). Without even physically visiting a museum, interested parties (researcher or non-professional) can peruse collections online, often accompanied by high-quality visual media, or even become fully immersed (see, for example, Museo Virtuale Della Cappadocia). The National Museum of Denmark maintains an online collection[52] of more than 500,000 images and objects from the museum collection. The Museo Arqueológico Nacional in Spain also maintains a robust search platform[53] with catalogue information and digital images of the collections. The British Museum[54] currently has available records representing four million objects, including more than one million records with one or more images. These images are published under a CC BY-NC-SA 4.0[55] licence, allowing them to be downloaded for free, edited and shared, as long they are properly attributed and are not used for commercial purposes.

Visitors to museums throughout Europe are also being introduced to new ways of engaging with archaeological content through digital mediations. Petersson and Larsson (2018), elaborating on Economou (2008), have outlined

---

[52] https://samlinger.natmus.dk/   [53] http://ceres.mcu.es/pages/AdvancedSearch?Museo=MAN
[54] https://www.britishmuseum.org/collection
[55] https://creativecommons.org/licenses/by-nc-sa/4.0/

three categories of digital museum experiences: informative screens, handheld devices, VR/immersive/3D solutions. As part of the collaborative Swedish Research Council Grant–funded project ARKDIS (Archaeological Information in the Digital Society), several museums in Sweden and Denmark were surveyed to determine how digital technologies impact the way archaeological concepts are constructed and conveyed to visitors. This survey highlighted the digital innovations adopted at these institutions. At the Danish Castle Centre in Vordingborg, for example, new exhibits are digitised and rely completely on handheld devices with headphones. Within the building, an object-centred exhibit is mediated by stories told through the devices. Outside, these devices utilise augmented reality (AR) to show the visitors parts of the Medieval building that are no longer standing (Petersson and Larsson 2018, 75–77). In addition, by utilising the traditional skills of museum heritage professionals and coupling them with new digital techniques, digitally immersive storytelling has been shown to engage visitors without compromising archaeological content. The Petroglyfiskt exhibit at the Österken Museum, Sweden, used motion capture to provide visitors with control over digital petroglyph characters, while a storytelling room used visuals and acoustic elements to convey information about Bronze Age cosmology (Petersson and Larsson 2018, 83–85). What is perhaps most exciting about the adoption of these digital technologies within museum and heritage contexts is that, as Pietroni (2016) discusses, they provide possibilities to re-configure cultural objects to enhance public understanding of the archaeological narrative. For more than a decade, the Istituto per le technologie applicate ai beni culturali (CNR ITABC)[56] worked to pioneer immersive museum experiences such as the Tiber Valley Virtual Museum (Pietroni 2016). Augmented and virtual reality are proving to be enormously useful in enhancing archaeological communication with the public, while expanding the reach of these narratives.

Outside museum contexts these technologies extend to the gamification of archaeological storytelling. For example, the Rome Reborn VR platform aims to make use of the generational appeal of immersive VR to educate. Going beyond the use of game platforms for education, recent years have seen a rising interest in archeogaming, as the archaeology of and in video games (Ezzeldin 2019; Reinhard 2016). These ever-expanding interfaces for conveying archaeological narratives have provided archaeologists in Europe with various avenues to further engage the public, as well as to target otherwise uninterested groups to whom these technologies may appeal.

The fastest growing and arguably the most widely practiced component of a digital public archaeology is taking place on the social web. The development

---

[56] http://www.itabc.cnr.it/

of Web 2.0 technology has allowed archaeologists in Europe and elsewhere to generate and publish their own content, while interacting directly with non-professionals. Perry and Beale define the social web as, 'parts of the Internet which are open to sharing content and information, structed in such a way that individuals can add to, edit, comment and remix content using a variety of interfaces' (2015, 154). These interfaces include, but are certainly not limited to, social networking sites like Twitter and Facebook, blogging sites like Wordpress and Blogspot, and even online gaming platforms (for a more complete list see Jeffrey 2012; Perry and Beale 2015). The benefit of these platforms for a European public archaeology is the direct interaction with the public where feedback can be immediate. Archaeologists and archaeological projects can communicate ideas, new finds, and research and excavation updates directly to an online community, be it colleagues or other interested groups. Whereas in the past these communications would have needed to be mediated through press releases or news media, the 'middle-man' is now removed. This type of one-way form of communication has been referred to as the 'broadcasting approach to digital engagement' (Bonacchi 2017, 66). One type of one-way communication, blogging, has provided an enormous opportunity to share self-published content across the European archaeological community. Blogs are often a peer-to-peer form of digital communication but still maintain an important role in archaeological knowledge making and sharing due to their dynamic and rapid content generation (Caraher and Reinhard 2015; Emery and Killgrove 2015; Morgan and Winter 2015).

Yet many social media platforms offer potential for more than a one-way street of interaction; these interfaces provide opportunities for dialogue between and within communities. Web 2.0 was unique, in part, from previous web technologies because of its participatory framework. Through social media, non-archaeologists can comment, engage with, and contribute to archaeological research and discussion. Twitter in particular provides an open platform for generating content and receiving feedback, which in the best-case scenario can lead to co-production of ideas. The broader archaeological community has used Twitter as a type of micro-blog for information and idea sharing, to publicise notable archaeological discoveries, or to reach existing archaeological communities (Richardson 2015). In addition to these uses, one recent endeavour has taken advantage of the openness of Twitter to address an issue in European archaeology (and elsewhere). Academic conferences are often limited to those who can afford the expense of travel and attendance, leaving out students, archaeologists who do not have access to institutional travel funds, professionals from lower-income regions, or individuals unable to travel for physical or other personal reasons. Further, almost none of the major professional conferences provide a space for the non-archaeological public to participate – listening, commenting, contributing. The Public Archaeology Twitter Conference (PATC)[57] began in 2017 to combat many of these issues and has since had three additional events (through 2020). The conference is held completely through Twitter, with participants allotted a fifteen-minute time slot to present their work through the platform's tools: text, image, meme, GIF. Although this model does not cure the issues that plague other conferences, it does offer an alternative mode of research presentation. The PATC model for conferences seems even more important considering the global Covid-19 pandemic, when archaeological conferences throughout the world were cancelled due to health and safety concerns.

Of course, the archaeological use of Twitter and other social media platforms is also susceptible to the same problems as any other use of these technologies. At the very least European archaeology has been slow to study and understand the full impact of the use of these media not only on the discipline, but also on the communities engaged with them (Perry and Beale 2015; Richardson 2013; 2018; Walker 2014). Like any technology adopted and employed by archaeologists, it is often difficult to see the long-term (or even medium term) ramifications of our use of, and research on, these platforms. Yet the potential ramifications of the social web may carry more weight than an inaccurate 3D artefact model, for example, if only because of the 'social' component of the research. On the one hand, public archaeology through social media can be incredibly useful because of the information that can be collected, and the underlying network structures used to better understand how people are interacting with content (Richardson 2019). However, as Lorna-Jane Richardson notes, the ethics of data privacy are very rarely considered (2018, 65–66). Due to the openness of platforms like Twitter, and the ability to use Application Programming Interfaces (APIs) to collect user data, there is often no explicit understanding by the user about how the data may be used, even if for purely research purposes related to public archaeology. Such practices may unintentionally reinforce neo-colonial archaeological practices. However, recent privacy restrictions of the largest social media platforms have significantly reduced researcher access to the APIs, which have in the past provided the necessary metadata for serious analytical research on social networks and heritage. Moving forward archaeologists focusing on social and digital archaeological research may have to utilise less restrictive data sources on the social web, like Wikipedia or Reddit (Richardson 2019).

Due to the openness of social media platforms, misunderstandings, misrepresentations, and overall harmful rhetoric is often attached to archaeological topics

---

[57] https://publicarchaeologyconference.wordpress.com/about/

without much intervention possible by archaeologists (see for example, Brophy 2018; Richardson and Booth 2017). The social web provides a place for pseudo-archaeological theories, far-right ideologies, hate speech, and 'trolling', in addition to its potential for participatory inclusion. Archaeologists are not immune to backlash on social media, as archaeological and heritage topics often factor heavily in modern life (Richardson 2018). In defending the depiction of black Roman soldiers in a BBC video to alt-right communities on Twitter, for example, esteemed Professor of Classics Mary Beard was treated to a barrage of insults on the platform that were rarely about her (correct) views but were primarily personal attacks (see her response here;[58] Brophy 2018). Ancient historian Sarah Bond faced similar online attacks for her story challenging the illusion of 'whiteness' on classical marble statuary (see original post Bond 2017;[59] response here).[60] And although social networking platforms do not have the sole claim on harassment via digital media (see Perry et al. 2015 for expanded discussion on the pervasiveness of harassment in the discipline), they act as powerful sites for such behaviours, drawing on the same qualities that make social media so useful for archaeological communication and collaboration. Archaeologists and those working with the ancient past are thus faced with the dilemma encountered often with the adoption of new technologies – do the negative repercussions that arise from enhanced public interaction outweigh the benefits of collaboration? In short, yes. But like any new aspect of the discipline, established infrastructure and best practices need to be developed to support and guide practitioners and, in this case, protect researchers from unintended harmful consequences.

In reviewing the public interaction with heritage through digital technologies, it is worth recognising that this interaction is not as democratising as archaeologists might hope. What is often taken for granted with the rapid development of an online infrastructure is the degree to which Internet access is still limited in many areas, including in Europe. Reviewing the European Commission 2019 report on the Use of Internet and Online Activities, we can see that in EU countries an average of only 65 per cent of Internet users participate regularly in online social networks (Figure 14). Additionally, the share of people in the EU who have never gone online was 11 per cent in 2018 (Figure 15). This includes larger proportions in Bulgaria (27%), Greece (25%), and Portugal (23%). Considering that the social web remains the largest component of a digital public archaeology in Europe, these statistics suggest an absence of a large portion of the population in the participation of online archaeological communities. There is little the discipline

---

[58] https://www.the-tls.co.uk/articles/roman-britain-black-white/

[59] https://hyperallergic.com/383776/why-we-need-to-start-seeing-the-classical-world-in-color/

[60] https://sarahemilybond.com/2017/04/30/the-argument-made-by-the-absence-on-whiteness-polychromy-and-diversity-in-classics/

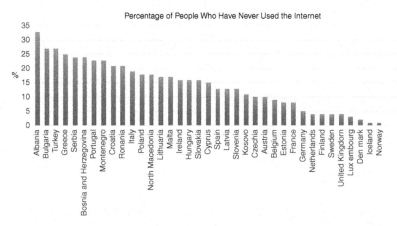

Figure 14 Graph showing percentage of EU countries' population who have never used the Internet (data from 2018).

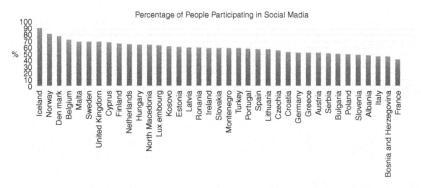

Figure 15 Graph showing percentage of EU countries' population who do not use social media (data from 2018).

can do to mitigate these numbers, but they reinforce the reality that archaeology remains embedded in broader social and economic contexts that reciprocally impact the connection between digital archaeology and the public. Fredheim (2020) has recently highlighted the reality that just because archaeological research is made 'open' to the public, that does not make it actually of or for the public. Fredheim notes that, 'while technology may remove some barriers to participation it also erects others. Crucially, technological advancements do little to change the reasons why archaeologists are interested in engaging with publics or how they view publics in terms of their capacity or expertise' (2020, 9). We must continue to use dialogues with the public through digital technology to embrace their potential to upend harmful practices of the discipline's past rather than sustain the status quo of traditional archaeological practices.

5.2 Community Archaeology

Though its precise definition is debated (Thomas 2017), the concept of community archaeology here refers to the active role of non-professionals in the creation and design of archaeological and heritage research. The communities involved can come from various places, as stakeholders need not only refer to those who live in a specific location or who claim to have a direct connection with the archaeological context. Participation in community archaeology is also heavily influenced by the laws and policies of each respective nation (Thomas 2017: 16).

Through the growing accessibility of digital media and techniques, recent projects have increasingly used these platforms to collaborate with different stakeholder groups in the production and co-production of archaeological information (Bollwerk 2015). One of the most comprehensive of these endeavours is the ACCORD project (Archaeological Community Co-Production of Research Resources). Beginning in 2013, the aim of the ACCORD project was to investigate the opportunities provided by digital visualisation technologies for community heritage practice (Jeffrey et al. 2015; Jones et al. 2018). Working with ten different community heritage groups throughout Scotland, the goal was to co-produce 3D digital – and in some cases physical – models of heritage places that were significant to the community groups (Jones et al. 2018, 5). The project, working in collaboration with these groups, used computational photogrammetry and RTI to create digital documentation of these meaningful places and monuments. Not only does this project provide a useful model for archaeological co-design and co-production through many of the stages of heritage work, it also responsibly managed the data produced through these community efforts. The resulting data produced by these groups are all available and archived through an ACCORD archive[61] by ADS. As addressed in Section 4, the long-term stability of archaeological data is vital to the future of European archaeology, community-based or otherwise.

Aligning with larger trends in web-based community building and distributive labour models, archaeological projects in Europe have also explored the practice of reaching out to communities through digital platforms for collaboration. We can actually look to the late 1990s for one example of digital collaboration between archaeologists and non-professionals: the Portable Antiquities Scheme (PAS).[62] Running in its current form for the last fifteen years, the PAS provides an open access database of finds in support of the Treasury Act (Bland et al. 2017). The PAS records archaeological finds discovered by the public, not including professional excavations, in England and Wales. The data available on the

---

[61] https://archaeologydataservice.ac.uk/archives/view/accord_ahrc_2015/overview.cfm
[62] https://finds.org.uk/about

database can be accessed by anyone, but exact findspots are only available to credentialed researchers. The current data consist of almost 1.5 million objects that often contain visual media in the form of photographs, illustrations, or 3D models, as well as linked data. This model of public–professional collaboration, coupled with an open access dissemination strategy, has proven productive. The PAS lists close to 150 PhD dissertations that have used their data, as well as more than 700 total research projects. The program, however, is not without its problems. It is limited by the scope of collaboration: heritage professionals and metal detectorists (or anyone who happens across an artefact). And although the scheme organises various outreach programs, the input on the creation of archaeological data remains limited – it is not truly inclusive. Additionally, there remains disagreement about the role of metal detectorists and the data reliability of such a program.

One project that was aimed at involving a wider group of non-professionals in data creation is the MicroPasts project. This collaborative project between the Institute of Archaeology, University College London and the British Museum was conceived as a model for public–institutional partnership in the creation of open archaeological or historical data, facilitated through crowd-sourced individual tasks (Bonacchi et al. 2014; 2015). Participants could contribute to a number of projects that included techniques such as photgrammetric image masking, translation, transcription, and YouTube video tagging. Coupled with MicroPasts' model for public inclusion in data creation was a crowd-funding platform. Beginning in 2014, MicroPasts provided opportunities for individuals to financially contribute to pre-approved archaeological projects, with mixed results (Bonacchi et al. 2015). Following a broader model of crowd-funded archaeology is the DigVentures[63] platform. This digital platform provides opportunities to participate in excavations through financial contributions. One can attend and participate in an excavation first-hand, watch live feeds and highlights from the excavations, or attend online courses on archaeology.

These different opportunities for community participation through digital platforms have expanded the reach of archaeologists and provide a foundation from which to expand community input in data creation, and eventually research design. By further developing infrastructures that can utilise the gamification aspects of user-generated data, the public may be drawn to heritage research and participation through enjoyable games that contribute useable research data. As possible models, we may look to participatory GIS projects (e.g., Harris 2012; Seitsonen 2017) or GlobalXplorer[64] (Yates 2018). We must then ask if this is where archaeologists should devote additional resources, and

---

[63] https://digventures.com/about-us/   [64] https://www.globalxplorer.org/about

if so, do these digital crowd-sourcing and funding efforts create more meaning-ful experiences for stakeholder groups with their heritage? There are important arguments against an economic model of archaeological crowd-funding. First, an acceptance of this model suggests that heritage work is now solely the purview of charity rather than a social service/need. If one must contribute financially to participate in archaeological projects, then access to cultural heritage becomes restricted (Sayer 2014). Second, relying on these models risks confusing 'neo-libertariansim' for the democratising potential of online networks (Perry and Beale 2015). Digitally crowd-sourced projects still retain an us/them divide that contributes only to the archaeologist's research question; the input from the public is mainly in the form of (unacknowledged and unpaid) labour. One way to address some of these criticisms may be reassessing how we design our archaeological research.

Often missing in projects that aim to involve public participation is a direct role for non-professionals in research design. Digitally mediated community and public archaeology suffer from a top-down approach to stakeholder participation, as does most public-facing research. In contrast to many of these trends, the previously mentioned ACCORD project worked with com-munity groups to identity meaningful sites of heritage to them, as opposed to sites being deemed meaningful by the archaeologists (Jones et al. 2018). They found co-designing these projects countered traditional power dynamics between archaeologist and non-professional and provided a space to re-evaluate these dynamics in archaeological research (Jones et al. 2018, 5–6). These power structures exist in all aspects of archaeology but are especially highlighted when we move to a more public, collaborative practice. It will take more of this deliberate project design collaboration to expand our understanding of what is archaeologically important to a community, and what types and uses of digital tools will succeed in engaging the public in cultural heritage. A workshop held in April 2019, organised by Francesca Dolcetti, Rachel Opitz, and Sara Perry and sponsored by the EU COST ACTION ARKWORK,[65] was aimed at examining User Experience (UX) Design in Archaeology and Heritage. As Sara Perry outlines, UX is an extremely important component in the future of the discipline and 'success of the discipline as a scholarly, profes-sional and pedagogical pursuit' (Perry 2019). The intent of the workshop was to experiment with the principles that underlie participatory design in the context of digital-mediated archaeological experiences. This type of approach brings in users of the digital products, as well as stakeholder groups, to the design phase of the digital experience. Each of the digital products and platforms mentioned

---

[65] https://www.arkwork.eu/

in this section could benefit from stakeholder input at the design level. Archaeological and cultural heritage digital content is often designed with archaeologists in mind, and how we would use the technology or platform if we were to interact with it. Unfortunately, this approach neglects the interests and needs of wider communities, tending to highlight what draws us as heritage professionals to archaeological content. As we move towards a more inclusive archaeological practice, these aspects of design will have to be further examined and integrated into our work.

One way to focus on the user experience of archaeological content is to acknowledge how people are affected by the past. In her impactful article, Sara Perry outlines a way of thinking of archaeology and cultural heritage as having the potential to *enchant* (2019). This enchantment, the ability to move, affect, or emotionally engage an individual through archaeology, can and should be generated for 'its potential for achieving the goals of a truly publicly-beneficial professional practice' (Perry 2019, 355). Through the EU Commission-funded EMOTIVE[66] project, the potential for generating archaeological enchantment through digital technologies was explored (Perry 2019, 363–66). The EMOTIVE project utilised an interdisciplinary group to develop digital tools and experiences for specialists and non-specialists that produce an emotional engagement with cultural heritage.

As digital technologies continue to provide archaeologists in Europe with additional ways to follow Wheeler's aim of a public archaeology, we will also have to continue to address the social and ethical impacts of these technologies. Archaeology and cultural heritage institutions exist within broader socio-economic structures and are thus impacted and influenced by systems, behaviours, and patterns outside our control. The adoption of interactive and immersive virtual exhibits in museums is still affected by the financial situation of these institutions. Social media interfaces extend the reach of archaeological professionals but at the same time open those professionals to harmful and aggressive communities. Crowd-sourced and -funded projects provide a level of participation across regional boundaries that expands the field to non-professionals, yet it also risks reinforcing traditional archaeologist–layperson power structures and a 'pay-to-play' model of cultural heritage. Despite these complications, what should strike us about projects such as those discussed is that digital technologies are providing archaeologists with endlessly creative avenues to assess and reassess our role as communicators of and participants in cultural heritage. These avenues expose a bright future for an archaeology with the public.

---

[66] https://emotiveproject.eu/

6 Digital Futures in European Archaeology

What will the archaeology of Europe look like in ten, twenty, or fifty years? Echoing Witmore (2009, 517), there is little excuse for archaeologists not to envision how we will be using and engaging with the archaeological record in the future. Although archaeologists have been consuming digital technologies for more than five decades, their continuing influence on European archaeology will only accelerate, as the Covid-19 crisis likely illustrates. These emerging technologies give us an opportunity to rethink and reframe archaeological paradigms in a deliberate and planned way rather than getting swept up in the excitement over the latest and greatest technology. Exciting possibilities for artificial intelligence, machine learning, or big data methods in archaeology should be approached critically, as should all the other tools discussed in this Element. It seems clear that there is a reciprocal relationship between the pervading theoretical paradigm in archaeology and the digital techniques used for research. By being conscious of this relationship we give ourselves some control over how the discipline will change in the next ten or fifty years.

6.1 Big Data and Machine Learning

Archaeology has more recently been following the larger trends in data analysis by starting to adopt a 'big data' approach to archaeological data. Big data refers not only to the quantity of information but the way in which the data are used. Traditionally big data is defined as being high-volume, high-velocity and/or high-variety, though more recently these qualities are understood in a relative way rather than an absolute way. Of course, across disciplines the concept of big data varies considerably (see Gattiglia 2015, 114), and qualifiers are often used to further refine it, such as thick or slow data. If we are to use the term big data to apply to archaeological information analysis, archaeologists should focus more on the process side rather than the scale of data, or as VanValkenburgh and Dufton argue, 'attend to the ways in which increasingly larger and higher resolution datasets are changing how archaeologists work in the present and how we think about the past' (2020, 52–53).

But do archaeologists have big data? As a comparison, ADS has about twenty-two terabytes of data stored in their archive (ADS Annual Report 2019) while Facebook generates about four petabytes of data a day. This means that Facebook generates more than 180 times the amount of data stored at ADS, but in a single day! Coupling the extreme quantities of data collected from social media, online retailers, and the growing infrastructure of the Internet of Things (IOT), we are creating an almost unimaginable amount of data that can be used in big data research. This comparison is merely intended to illustrate how small archaeological datasets are compared to those that have spurred innovations in big data research. The larger the dataset is, the more one is able to mitigate bias and sampling errors. But archaeological data is usually never big enough to do this, which should give archaeologists pause.

With that said, archaeological data are increasing at an exponential rate, especially with regard to aerial images, GIS, and 3D data, and the methods developed in ICT and the natural sciences that may be usefully applied to archaeology. Geospatial data is one area of archaeological research that already deals with large amounts of data, with the demonstrated potential for linking together data across sites and regions (see McCoy 2017). Using aggregated geospatial datasets may provide new opportunities to recognise large-scale patterning through visualisations or statistical modelling. The same applies to large numbers of georeferenced aerial images (VanValkenburgh and Dufton 2020). The potential for geospatial big data in archaeology is in part limited by the restrictions required by these data, to protect cultural heritage from exploitation.

The potential for some of these methods in European archaeology has also been demonstrated in a number of zooarchaeological projects (see for example Arbuckle et al. 2014; Connolly et al. 2011; Orton et al. 2016). One can also look to the English Landscape and Identities Project (EngLaID), which collected digital archaeological data spanning the period from 1500 BC to AD 1086 in England (Cooper and Green 2016). The aim was to create a landscape history of England through this time frame, using published and digital data. More than one million text records were compiled to create the basis for this project, bringing together a wide range of sources. However, in addition to illustrating the potential for collecting large, distinct datasets, it also demonstrates one issue with approaching archaeology through a big data lens: archaeological data is complex, filled with biases in recording, categorisation and classification, accessibility, and the archaeological record itself (Cooper and Green 2016). Not only do we have to contend with the difference in archaeological practices for excavation or data recording across international borders (or even within) and the lack of standardisation that accompanies it, but also the reality that changing practices of excavation throughout time have created uneven datasets, making the act of even aggregating big archaeological data difficult (Löwenborg 2018, 49). When dealing with these data we must also understand the nature of the archaeological record as it relates to the way we construct the past. As Huggett recently observed,

> The correlations we find in archaeology do not explain cultural process because they are several steps removed from human practice: effectively we employ proxy data as a means of accessing the immaterial processes behind the tangible evidence we have to hand (visibility as a proxy for knowledge in GIS, or friction as a proxy for accessibility, artefact density for levels of human

activity, radiocarbon plots for prehistoric occupation, tombs as indicators of settlement, material culture traits as proxies for social identity and/or group membership, or trade and exchange, and so on) (2020, 514).

Huggett's critique of a big data approach to archaeological research reveals that because of the complexities inherent in archaeological data, and the reality that the data produced in archaeology are proxies for cultural processes, we must be wary of the data-driven approach that typically accompanies big data analyses. We should also be aware of the potential for de-humanising archaeological data by creating such a distance between outputs (broad interpretations about the past from big data) and the people who lived in the past and whose behaviours produced the archaeological record. It is not just ancient people who are removed from a data-driven approach to archaeology, but contemporary stakeholders as well. Mickel (2020) and Gupta et al. (2020) have all highlighted missing pieces of big data approaches in archaeology: the inability to integrate proximity[67] or indigenous (or other stakeholder) rights to big data. Due to all these critiques, it remains to be seen if the discipline will continue on the track towards big data approaches, or if that is even a direction it should be going.

The datafication that has spurred big data approaches in archaeology has also opened possibilities for advances in machine learning applications in the discipline. Machine learning algorithms use sample or 'training' datasets to create mathematical models to make predictions about a new dataset. This process is essentially what archaeologists are doing on a regular basis in our analyses; our previous knowledge of pottery styles and form allow us to classify a newly uncovered sherd, or our experience identifying features on the landscape allows us to discover new features through satellite imagery. Machine learning automates this process in archaeology and some recent applications of these methods show very interesting results. Landscape feature detection has been one area of machine learning research that has been used for some time in archaeology, first with aerial and satellite imagery and more recently with airborne LiDAR datasets (see Davis 2019 for comprehensive discussion of past uses). The latest innovation in this type of machine learning application is the addition of deep neural network approaches to archaeological prospection, which allow automated object detection on enormous amounts of topographic data (Trier et al. 2019; Verschoof-van der Vaart and Lambers 2019).

A recently completed project, ArchAIDE, shows the potential for machine learning to influence an even wider archaeological audience by automating the essential classification of pottery (Anichini et al. 2020). A mobile app was

---

[67] Defined as local expertise – the long-term, multi-sensory connection local communities have with archaeological sites and landscapes.

developed through this project that allows users to take a photo of a pottery sherd, which is then compared to a massive database of pottery (the 'training' data) by image recognition algorithms. The resulting output is a classification of the pottery based on the types in the database (Anichini et al. 2020). This type of automated research opens significant possibilities for archaeologists, saving time in the classification process and refining accuracy in research. However, a barrier to these applications becoming widespread across regions is the time it takes to create the original sample data. It was noted that the ArchAIDE team struggled to find more than ten examples per ceramic type to train the system, a minimum for the system to develop (Anichini et al. 2020). If this is to become a widespread and accurate tool in European archaeology, the training dataset needs to be enormous, with extensive temporal and geographical coverage. It also returns us to the issue of 'black boxing' in archaeological technologies. These examples of machine learning remove the interpretive element to site, feature, and artefact recognition. If indeed classification of artefacts and arch-aeological features rests at the heart of archaeological practice, are we okay with removing ourselves from that process?

6.2 Sustainability

Although the future of European archaeology may rest with computer automa-tion, the direct role we have as citizens of the world is an even more meaningful aspect of archaeological futures. The environmental impact of the influx of large amounts of data in archaeological work is rarely discussed. Energy is required to power all aspects of digital archaeology, from the computer and digital camera to the data centres that house servers maintaining cloud data. Powering data centres requires huge amounts of energy, due in part to the fact they have to run all day, every day, and because they have to use very intricate cooling systems. It is estimated that in 2020, European data centres will consume 104 twh/year, equal to about 4 per cent of total energy consumption in the EU (Bertoldi et al. 2017).[68] Fossil fuels, which are still responsible for a large majority of the world's energy, are the primary fuel source for these data centres. Archaeological work is not responsible for any significant portion of this data processing, to be sure, however, we are contributing something. Archaeology does not exist in a social vacuum, and as producers and users of large quantities of digital data we should be aware of the issues of sustainabil-ity – sustainability not only of the data we produce but also of the physical

---

[68] Initiatives through the Climate Change Agreement and the European Commission's Code of Conduct for Data Centre Energy Efficiency will hopefully address some issues of energy consumption.

infrastructures that maintain those data. In thinking about the future of the discipline we will have to consider our role in the massive energy consumption resulting from the practice of digital archaeology.

Another aspect of sustainable practices in archaeology that is rarely considered is the impact of global economic markets on our ability to continue to develop as a digital discipline at this pace. Although not all the techniques and tools discussed in this Element are limited by their cost, many are. All sectors of archaeological work can be negatively impacted by economic recessions or austerity policies; limited funding to universities and museums and shrinking infrastructure development that funds contract archaeology all affect the ability of archaeologists to continue (or begin) utilising digital tools in different aspects of their work. We can look to the early 2000s for evidence of this impact, to the end of the 'Celtic Tiger' economy in Ireland. The massive infrastructure development in the late 1990s and early 2000s fuelled expansive archaeological work in the country, but following the downturn in 2003, and especially the global recession in 2008, many contract companies did not survive. As a result, much of the data was left unpublished. Archaeology, like many humanities and social sciences, is often at the mercy of larger economic trends, and the economic impact that Covid-19 will have on the discipline is yet to be seen. It is a reality that will unfortunately need to be on our minds as we transition to using more financially demanding digital tools.

6.3 Conclusion

As the discussion of sustainability shows us, computers are not just tools that exist in isolation. As Cook and Compton rightly point out, 'digital technologies are indeed tools, but they are not neutral or passive and therefore the technological ecosystem within which archaeology functions must be connected to broader paradigmatic shifts' (2018, 38). We have already seen through time that the development of digital tools has accompanied shifts in theoretical paradigms (Chenhall 1968; Lock 2003). Very early computer use in archaeology, based on statistical computing and data recording, accompanied a change from a culture historical focus to more quantitative or processual approaches to archaeology. With the increased access to computers through microprocessors, we saw a shift to alternate archaeological narratives by expanding who is 'in charge' of creating archaeological knowledge. Currently, with the extreme proliferation of data, connecting across platforms and nations, we may be returning in some ways to a more quantitative focus – trying to reconstruct the past with the sheer quantity of information and data-driven approaches. At the same time the use of digital technologies has also paralleled the importance of inclusive archaeological frameworks, like feminist, post-colonial, indigenous, or queer discourses. There is great potential for harnessing digital tools for disrupting traditional archaeological structures and re-defining what inclusion means in archaeology, but there is also a danger of reinforcing existing inequalities and introducing new forms of harassment (Cook 2019). It remains important that we be purposeful in the use of these tools, in whatever context they are employed, and it is necessary to be aware of the intricate role the technology plays in our archaeological practices.

In his 1968 article reviewing the role of computers in archaeology, Chenhall described how many archaeologists have not yet come to understand the potential usefulness of computers in archaeological work. He says, 'Some of them still look upon the computer as a sort of magic black box – which it is not' (Chenhall 1968, 161). I would argue that this view is still present in archaeology, and it has even grown over the past five decades. The increased use of applications with graphical user interfaces (GUI) during this period meant that we did not have to learn *what* the computer was doing as long as it worked – can we input our data and get out some product? It is because of this that we view digital technologies with a near reverence, 'knowing' that they work in objective ways despite not knowing how they work. What does this separation from process do to our experience with archaeology and archaeological research? Throughout this Element examples have shown the increasing estrangement of the archaeologist from the traditional practices of archaeology. These traditional practices are supplemented or supplanted by new skills that make use of amazing advances in hardware and software. This increased reliance on a black box is not just archaeological but our state in the world. Perhaps our continuing relationship with the digital is neither a positive nor a negative for our epistemic practice, just the way digital society is taking us.

The ways that new tools alter archaeological research have been highlighted throughout this Element; digital visualisations provide immense potential for rethinking archaeological excavations and physical cultural heritage; data accessibility and interoperability create new worlds for reuse and re-contextualisation of archaeological information; digital platforms can act as conduits for increased attention to public and community connections. At the same time the continued use of these tools forms a dialectical relationship with traditional archaeological structures. That is, changing theoretical paradigms in archaeological work influence, and are influenced by, innovations in digital technologies. The future of European archaeology will continue to be shaped by the digital world in ways we are unlikely to predict. But we can do our best to use these technologies to shape the discipline in ways that we would prefer to see it go.

Bibliography

Alaguero, M., Bustillo, A., Guinea B. & Iglesias, L. (2015). The virtual reconstruction of a small Medieval town: the case of Briviesca (Spain). In F. Giligny, F. Djindjian, L. Costa, P. Moscati, & S. Robert, eds. *CAA2014 21st Century Archaeology: Concepts, Methods, and Tools. Proceedings of the 42nd Annual Conference on Computer Applications and Quantitative Methods in Archaeology.* Oxford: Archeopress, pp. 575–84.

Aloia, N., Binding, C., Cuy, S., Doerr, M., Fanini, B., Felicetti, A., Fihn, J., Gavrilis, D., Geser, G., Hollander, H., Meghini, C., Niccolucci, F., Nurra, F., Papatheodorou, C., Richards, J., Ronzino, P., Scopigno, R., Theodoridou, M., Tudhope, D., Vlachidis, A. & Wright, H. (2017). ARIADNE: a European research e-infrastructure for archaeology. *Journal of Computing and Cultural Heritage* 10.3.

Amico, F. Ronzino, P., Vassallo, V., Miltiadous, N., Hermon, S. & Niccolucci, F. (2018). Theorizing authenticity – practising reality: the 3D replica of the Kazaphani boat. In P. Di Giuseppantonio Di Franco, F. Galeazzi & V. Vassallo, eds. *Authenticity and Cultural Heritage in the Age of 3D Digital Reproductions.* Cambridge: McDonald Institute for Archaeological Research, pp. 111–22.

Anichini, F., Banterle, F., Garrigós, J. B. et al. (2020). Developing the ArchAIDE application: a digital workflow for identifying, organising and sharing archaeological pottery using automated image recognition. *Internet Archaeology* 52. https://doi.org/10.11141/ia.52.7

Arbuckle, B. S., Kansa, S. W., Kansa, E. et al. (2014). Data sharing reveals complexity in the westward spread of domestica animals across Neolithic Turkey. *PLoS ONE* 9, e99845.

Averett, E., Gordon, J. & Counts, D., eds. (2016). *Mobilizing the Past for a Digital Future: The Potential of Digital Archaeology.* Grand Forks: Digital Press, University of North Dakota.

Beale, G. & Beale, N. (2015). Community-driven approaches to open source archaeological imaging. In A. T. Wilson & B. Edwards, eds. *Open Source Archaeology: Ethics and Practice.* Berlin: De Gruyter Open, pp. 44–63.

Beard, M. (1994). Casts and cast-offs: the origins of the Museum of Classical Archaeology. *Proceedings of the Cambridge Philological Society* 39, 1–29.

Beck, A. & Neylon, C. (2012). A vision for open archaeology. *World Archaeology* 44(4), 479–97.

Benjamin, W. (1968) [1935]. The work of art in the age of mechanical reproduction. In W. Benjamin, ed. *Illuminations. Essays and Reflections.* New York: Harcourt, Brace & World, Inc.

Bennett, R. (2014). Airborne laser scanning for archaeological prospection. In F. Remondion & S. Campana, eds. *3D Recording and Modelling in Archaeology and Cultural Heritage: Theory and Best Practices.* BAR International Series 2598. Archeopress: Oxford, pp. 25–36.

Berners-Lee, T. (2006). Linked data. www.w3.org/DesignIssues/LinkedData .html

Bertoldi, P., M. Avgerinou & Castellazzi, L. (2017). *Trends in data centre energy consumption under the European Code of Conduct for Data Centre Energy Efficiency.* JRC Technical Report, European Commission.

Bevan, A. (2015). The data deluge. *Antiquity* 89(348), 1473–84.

Bishara. H. (2019, November 26). Official 3D scans of Nefertiti bust are released after three-year battle. *Hyperallergic.* https://hyperallergic.com/530400/offi cial-3d-scans-of-nefertiti-bust-are-released-after-three-year-battle

Blackwell, A. H. & Blackwell, C. W. (2013). Hijacking shared heritage: cultural artifacts and intellectual property rights. *Chicago-Kent Journal of Intellectual Property* 13(1), 137–64.

Bland, R., Lewis, M., Pett, D., Richardson, I., Robbins, K. & Webley, R. (2017). The Treasure Act and Portable Antiquities Scheme in England and Wales. In G. Moshenska, ed. *Key Concepts in Public Archaeology.* London: UCL Press, pp. 107–21.

Bohrer, F. N. (2011). *Photography and Archaeology.* London: Reaktion Books Ltd. Oxbow Books.

Bollwerk, E. (2015). Co-creation's role in digital public archaeology. *Advances in Archaeological Practice* 3(3), 223–34.

Bonacchi, C. (2017). Digital media in public archaeology. In G. Moshenska, ed. *Key Concepts in Public Archaeology.* London: UCL Press, pp. 60–72.

Bonacchi C., Bevan, A., Pett, D., Keinan-Schoonbaert, A., Sparks, R., Wexler, J. & Wilkin, N. (2014). Crowd-sourced archaeological research: the MicroPasts Project. *Archaeology International* 17, 61–68.

Bonacchi, C., Pett, D., Bevan, A. & Keinan-Schoonbaert, A. (2015). Experiments in crowd-funding community archaeology. *Journal of Community Archaeology & Heritage* 2(3), 184–98.

Bond, S. (2017, June 7). Why we need to start seeing the classical world in color. *Hyperallergic.* https://hyperallergic.com/383776/why-we-need-to-start-seeing-the-classical-world-in-color

Bourdieu, P. (1996). *Photography: A Middle-brow Art.* Stanford: Stanford University Press.

Brophy, K. (2018). The Brexit hypothesis and prehistory. *Antiquity* 92(366), 1650–58.

Brown, B. J., Toler-Franklin, C., Nehab, D. et al. (2008). A system for high-volume acquisition and matching of fresco fragments: reassembling Theran wall paintings. *ACM Transactions on Graphics (TOG) (Proceedings of ACM SIGGRAPH 2008)* 27(3): article no. 84.

Caraher, W. (2013). Slow archaeology. *North Dakota Quarterly* 80(2), 43–52.

Caraher, W. (2016). Slow archaeology: technology, efficiency, and archaeology work. In E. W. Averett, J. Gordon & D. Counts, eds. *Mobilizing the Past for a Digital Future: The Potential of Digital Archaeology*. Grand Forks: Digital Press, University of North Dakota, pp. 421–41.

Caraher, W. & Reinhard, A. (2015). From blogs to books: blogging as community, practice and platform. *Internet Archaeology* 39. https://doi.org/10.11141/ia.39.7

Champion, E. & Rahaman, H. (2020). Survey of 3D digital heritage repositories and platforms. *Virtual Archaeology Review* 11(23), 1–15.

Chenhall, R. G. (1967). The description of archaeological data in computer language. *American Antiquity* 32(2), 161–67.

Chenhall, R. G. (1968). The impact of computers on archaeological theory: an appraisal and projection. *Computers and the Humanities* 3(1), 15–24.

Chenhall, R. G. (1971). The archaeological data bank: a progress report. *Computers and the Humanities* 5(3), 159–69.

Connolly, J. et al. (2011). Meta-analysis of zooarchaeological data from SW Asia and SE Europe provides insight into the origins and spread of animal husbandry. *Journal of Archaeological Science* 38, 538–45.

Cook, K. (2019). EmboDIYing disruption: queer, feminist and inclusive digital archaeologies. *European Journal of Archaeology* 22(3), 398–414.

Cook, K. & Compton, M. E. (2018). Canadian digital archaeology: on boundaries and futures. *Canadian Journal of Archaeology* 42, 38–45.

Cooney, G. (2006). Newgrange – a view from the platform. *Antiquity* 80(309), 697–708.

Cooper, A. & Green, C. (2016). Embracing the complexities of 'big data' in archaeology: the case of the English Landscape and Identities Project. *Journal of Archaeological Method and Theory* 23, 271–304.

Corns, A. & Shaw, R. (2013). Lidar and world heritage sites in Ireland: why was such a rich data sources gathered, how is it being utilised, and what lessons have been learned? In R. S. Opitz & D. C. Cowley, eds. *Interpreting Archaeological Topography: 3D Data, Visualisation and Observation*. Oxbow Books, Oxford, pp. 146–60.

Costopoulos, A. (2016). Digital Archeology Is Here (and Has Been for a While). *Frontiers in Digital Humanities*. https://doi.org/10.3389/fdigh.2016.00004

Counts, D. B., Averett, E. W. & Garstki, K. (2016). A fragmented past: (re) constructing antiquity through 3D artefact modelling and customised structured light scanning at Athienou-*Malloura*, Cyprus. *Antiquity* 90(349), 206–18.

Counts, D. B., Averett, E. W., Garstki, K. & Toumazou, M. K. (2020). *Visualizing Votive Practice: Exploring Limestone and Terracotta Sculpture from Athienou-Malloura through 3D Models*. Grand Forks: The Digital Press at the University of North Dakota.

Cowgill, G. L. (1967). Computer applications in archaeology. *Computers and the Humanities* 2(1), 17–23.

Dallas, C. (2016). Jean-Claude Gardin on archaeological data, representation and knowledge: implications for digital archaeology. *Journal of Archaeological Method and Theory* 23, 305–30.

D'Andrea, A. & Fernie, K. (2013). CARARE 2.0: a metadata schema for 3D cultural objects. In *2013 Digital Heritage International Congress (Digital Heritage)* vol. 2, pp. 137–43. IEEE, 2013.

Davis, D. (2019). Object-based image analysis: a review of developments and future directions of automated feature detection in landscape archaeology. *Archaeological Prospection* 26, 155–63

Davis, S., Brady, C., Megarry, W. & Barton, K. (2013). Lidar survey in the Brú na Bóinne world heritage site. In R. S. Opitz and D. C. Cowley, eds. *Interpreting Archaeological Topography: 3D Data, Visualisation and Observation*. Oxbow Books, Oxford, pp. 223–37.

Davis, S., Rassmann, K. & Bánffy, E. (2019). Filling in the gaps in Brú na Bóinne. *Archaeology Ireland* 33(3), 22–24.

Dell'Unto, N. (2014). The use of 3D models for intra-site investigation in archaeology. In F. Remondion & S. Campana, eds. *3D Recording and Modelling in Archaeology and Cultural Heritage: Theory and best practices*. BAR International Series 2598. Archeopress: Oxford, pp. 151–58.

Dell'Unto, N. (2018). 3D models and knowledge production. In I. Huvila, ed. *Archaeology and Archaeological Information in the Digital Society*. London: Routledge, pp. 54–69.

Demesticha S., Skarlatos, D. & Neophytou, A. (2014). The 4th-century B.C. shipwreck at Mazotos, Cyprus: new techniques and methodologies in the 3D mapping of shipwreck excavations. *Journal of Field Archaeology* 39, 134–50.

De Reu, J., De Smedt, P., Herremans, D., Van Meirvenne, M., Laloo, P. & De Clercq, W. (2014). On introducing an image-based 3D reconstruction method in archaeological excavation practice. *Journal of Archaeological Science* 41, 251–262.

De Reu, J., Plets, G., Verhoeven, G., De Smedt, P., Bats, M., Cherretté, B., De Maeyer, W., Deconynck, J., Herremans, D., Laloo, P., Van Meirvenne, M. & De Clercq, D. (2013). Towards a three-dimensional cost-effective registration of the archaeological heritage. *Journal of Archaeological Science* 40, 1108–21.

Diaz-Guardamino, M., Sanjuán, L. G., Wheatly, D. & Zamora, V. R. (2015). RTI and the study of engraved rock art: a re-examination of the Iberian south-western stelae of Setefilla and Almadén de la Plata 2 (Seville, Spain). *Digital Applications in Archaeology and Cultural Heritage* 2, 41–54.

Di Guiseppantonio Di Franco, P., Galeazzi, F. & Camporesi, C. (2012). 3D Virtual Dig: a 3D Application for Teaching Fieldwork in Archaeology. *Internet Archaeology* 32. DOI: 10.11141/ia.32.4

Di Giuseppantonio Di Franco, P. , Galeazzi, F. & Vassalo, V., eds. (2018a). *Authenticity and Cultural Heritage in the Age of 3D Digital Reproductions*. Cambridge: McDonald Institute for Archaeological Research.

Di Giuseppantonio Di Franco, P., Galeazzi, F. & Vassalo, V. (2018b). Introduction: why authenticity still matters today. In P. Di Giuseppantonio Di Franco, F. Galeazzi, & V. Vassallo, eds. *Authenticity and Cultural Heritage in the Age of 3D Digital Reproductions*. Cambridge: McDonald Institute for Archaeological Research, pp. 49–56.

Di Giuseppantonio Di Franco, P. , Matthews, J. L. & Matlock, T. (2016). Framing the past: how virtual experience affects bodily description of artefacts. *Journal of Cultural Heritage* 17, 179–87.

Djindjian, F. (2009). The golden years for mathematics and computers in archaeology (1965–1985). *Archeologia e Calcolatori* 20, 61–73.

Djindjian, F. (2019). Archaeology and computers: a long story in the making of modern archaeology. *Archeologia e Calcolatori* 30, 13–20.

Doneus, M. & Kühteiber, T. (2013). Airborne laser scanning and archaeological interpretation – bringing back the people. In R. S. Opitz & D. C. Cowley, eds. *Interpreting Archaeological Topography: 3D Data, Visualisation and Observation*. Oxbow Books, Oxford, pp. 32–50.

Doran, J. E. & Hodson, F. R. (1975). *Mathematics and Computers in Archaeology*. Cambridge: Harvard University Press.

Ducke, B. (2012). Natives of a connected world: free and open source software in archaeology. *World Archaeology* 44(4), 571–79.

Ducke. B. (2015). Free and open source software in commercial and academic archaeology: sustainable investments and reproducible research. In A. T. Wilson & B. Edwards, eds. *Open Source Archaeology: Ethics and Practice* Berlin: De Gruyter Open, pp. 92–110.

Dufton, J. A. (2016). CSS for success? Some thoughts on adapting the browser-based archaeological recording kit (ARK) for mobile recording. In E. W. Averett, J. Gordon, & D. Counts, eds. *Mobilizing the Past for a Digital Future: The Potential of Digital Archaeology.* Grand Forks: Digital Press, University of North Dakota, pp. 373–98.

Đuričić, S. (2017). Physical vs. virtual reconstruction. In N. Tasić, P. Novaković, & M. Horňák, eds. *Virtual Reconstructions and Computer Visualisations in Archaeological practice*, CONPRA Series, Vol. IV. University of Ljubljana Press, Faculty of Arts.

Earl, G., Martinez, K. & Malzbender, T. (2010). Archaeological applications of polynomial texture mapping: analysis, conservations and representation. *Journal of Archaeological Science* 37, 2040–50.

Economou, M. (2008). A world of interactive exhibits. In P. F. Marty & K. B. Jones, eds. *Museum Informatics. People, Information, and Technology in Museums.* New York: Routledge, pp. 242–60.

Edwards, B. & Wilson, A. T. (2015). Open archaeology: definitions, challenges and context. In A. T. Wilson & B. Edwards, eds. *Open Source Archaeology: Ethics and Practice* Berlin: De Gruyter Open, pp. 1–5.

Ellenberger, K. (2017). Virtual and augmented reality in public archaeology teaching. *Advances in Archaeological Practices* 5(3), 305-9.

Elliot, T., Heath, S. & Muccigrosso, J. (2014). Prologue and Introduction. *ISAW Papers* 7.1. http://dlib.nyu.edu/awdl/isaw/isaw-papers/7/elliott-heath-muccigrosso

Ellis, S. (2016). Are we ready for new (digital) ways to record archaeological fieldwork? A case study from Pompeii. In E. W. Averett, J. Gordon, & D. Counts, eds. *Mobilizing the Past for a Digital Future: The Potential of Digital Archaeology.* Grand Forks: Digital Press, University of North Dakota, pp. 51–76.

Emery, K. M. & Killgrove, K. (2015). Bones, bodies, and blogs: outreach and engagement in bioarchaeology. *Internet Archaeology* 39. http://dx.doi.org/10.11141/ia.39.5

Eriksen, P. (2004). Newgrange og den hvide mur. *Kuml*, 45–77.

Eriksen, P. (2006). The rolling stones from Newgrange. *Antiquity* 80(309), 709–10.

Eve, S. (2018). The embodied GIS. Using mixed reality to explore multi-sensory archaeological landscapes. *Internet Archaeology* 44. https://doi.org/10.11141/ia.44.3

Eve, S. (2018). Losing our senses, an exploration of 3D object scanning. *Open Archaeology* 4. https://doi.org/10.1515/opar-2018-0007

Ezzeldin, A. (2019). Archaeogaming as public archaeology. In H. Williams, C. Pudney & A. Ezzeldin, eds. *Public Archaeology: Arts of Engagement.* Oxford: Archaeopress, Access Archaeology, pp. 200–205

Faniel, I. M., Austin, A., Kansa, E., Kansa, S. W., France, P., Jacobs, J., Boytner, R. & Yakel, W. (2018). Beyond the archive: Bridging data creation and reuse in archaeology. *Advances in Archaeological Practice* 6(2), 105–16.

Fee, S. (2013). Reflections on custom mobile app developments for archaeological data collection. In E. W. Averett, J. Gordon & D. Counts, eds. *Mobilizing the Past for a Digital Future: The Potential of Digital Archaeology.* Grand Forks: Digital Press, University of North Dakota, pp. 221–36.

Fleury, P., Madeleine, S. & Lefèvre, N. (2015). Forum Romanum: a 3D model for self-service educational purposes. In F. Giligny, F. Djindjian, L. Costa, P. Moscati & S. Robert, eds. *CAA2014 21st Century Archaeology: Concepts, Methods, and Tools. Proceedings of the 42nd Annual Conference on Computer Applications and Quantitative Methods in Archaeology.* Archeopress, pp. 569–74.

Forte, M. (2014). 3D archaeology: new perspectives and challenges – the example of Çatalhöyük. *Journal of Eastern Mediterranean Archaeology and Heritage Studies* 2(1), 1–29.

Forte, M. & Siliotti, A., eds. (1997). *Virtual Archaeology. Great Discoveries Brought to Life Through Virtual Reality.* London: Thames and Hudson.

Fredheim, L. H. (2020). Decoupling 'open' and 'ethical' archaeologies: rethinking deficits and expertise for ethical public participation in archaeology and heritage. *Norwegian Archaeological Review.* https://doi.org/10.1080/00293652.2020.1738540

Galeazzi, F., Caillieri, M., Dellepiane, M., Charno, M., Richards, J. & Scopigno, R. (2016). Web-based visualization of 3D data in archaeology: The ADS 3D viewer. *Journal of Archaeological Science: Reports* 9, 1–11.

Gardin, J.-C. (1971). Archaeology and computers: new perspectives. *International Social Science Journal* 23(2), 189–203.

Gardin, J.-C. (1980). *Archaeological Constructs: An Aspect of Theoretical Archaeology.* Cambridge: Cambridge University Press.

Garstki, K. (2017). Virtual representation: the production of 3D digital artifacts. *Journal of Archaeological Method and Theory* 24, 726–50.

Garstki, K. (2018). Virtual authority and the expanding role of 3D digital artifacts. In P. Di Giuseppantonio Di Franco, F. Galeazzi, & V. Vassallo, eds. *Authenticity and Cultural Heritage in the Age of 3D Digital Reproductions.* Cambridge: McDonald Institute for Archaeological Research, pp. 75–82.

Garstki, K., Larkee, C. & LaDisa, J. (2019). A role for immersive visualization experiences in teaching archaeology. *Studies in Digital Heritage* 3(1), 46–59.

Garstki, K., Schulenburg, M. & Cook, R. A. (2018). Practical application of digital photogrammetry for fieldwork in the American Midwest: an example from the Middle Ohio Valley. *Midcontinental Journal of Archaeology* 43 (2), 133–50.

Gattiglia, G. (2015). Think big about data: archaeology and the big data challenge. *Archäologische Informationen*, 38, 113–24.

Geser, G. (2016). *WP15 study: towards a web of archaeological linked open data*. ARIADNE Report, European Commission.

Gordon, J. M., Averett, E. W. & Counts, D. B. (2016). Mobile computing in archaeology: exploring and interpreting current practices. In E. Averett, J. Gordon, & D. Counts, eds. *Mobilizing the Past for a Digital Future: The Potential of Digital Archaeology*. Grand Forks: Digital Press, University of North Dakota. pp. 1–32.

Graham, S., N. Gupta, J. Smith et al. (2019). *The Open Digital Archaeology Textbook*. https://o-date.github.io/draft/book/index.html

Green, S. Bevan, A. & Shapland, M. (2014). A comparative assessment of structure from motion methods for archaeological research. *Journal of Archaeological Science* 46, 173–81.

Gupta, N., Blair, S. & Nicholas, R. (2020). What we see, what we don't see: data governance, archaeological spatial databases and the rights of indigenous peoples in an age of big data. *Journal of Field Archaeology* 45 (Sup 1), S39–S50.

Harris, T. M. (2012). Interfacing archaeology and the world of citizen sensors: exploring the impact of neogeography and volunteered geographic information on an authenticated archaeology. *World Archaeology* 44(4), 580–91.

Hermon, S. & Niccolucci, F. (2018). Digital authenticity and the London Charter. In P. Di Giuseppantonio Di Franco, F. Galeazzi, & V. Vassallo, eds. *Authenticity and Cultural Heritage in the Age of 3D Digital Reproductions*. Cambridge: McDonald Institute for Archaeological Research, pp. 37–48.

Hill A. C., Rowan, Y. & Kersel, M. (2014). Mapping with aerial photographs: recording the past, the present, and the invisible at Marj Rabba, Israel. *Near Eastern Archaeology* 77, 182–86.

Hopkinson, G. & Winters, J. (2003). Problems with permatrace: a note on digital image publication. *Internet Archaeology* 14. https://doi.org/10.11141/ia.14.5

Horňák, M. (2017). Examples of good practice in 3D visualization in preventive archaeology. In N. Tasić, P. Novaković, & M. Horňák, eds. *Virtual Reconstructions and Computer Visualisations in Archaeological Practice, CONPRA Series, Vol. IV*. University of Ljubljana Press, Faculty of Arts, pp. 49–68.

Howland, M. D., Kuester, F. & Levy, T. E. (2014). Structure from motion: twenty-first century field recording with 3D technology. *Near Eastern Archaeology* 77(3), 187–91.

Huggett, J. (2012). Lost in information? Ways of knowing and modes of representation in e-archaeology. *World Archaeology* 44(4), 538–52.

Huggett, J. (2016, April 8). A digital detox for digital archaeology [Blog post]. http://introspectivedigitalarchaeology.com/2016/04/08/a-digital-detox-for-digital-archaeology/#more-317

Huggett, J. (2020). Is big digital data different? Towards a new archaeological paradigm. *Journal of Field Archaeology* 45(Sup 1), S8–S17.

Huvila, I. (2018). Introduction. In Huvila, I., eds. *Archaeology and Archaeological Information in the Digital Society.* London, Routledge. pp. 1–13.

Jaklič, A., Erič, M., Mihajlović, I., Stopinšek, Ž. & Solina, F. (2015). Volumetric models from 3D point clouds: the case study of Sarcophagi Cargo from a 2nd/3rd century AD Roman shipwreck near Sutivan on island Brač, Croatia. *Journal of Archaeological Science* 62, 143–52.

Jeffrey, S. (2012). A new Digital Dark Age? Collaborative web tools, social media and long-term preservation. *World Archaeology* 44(4), 553–70.

Jeffrey, S. (2015). Challenging heritage visualisation: beauty, aura and democratisation. *Open Archaeology* 1, 144–52.

Jeffrey, S. (2018). Digital heritage objects, authorship, ownership and engagement. In P. Di Giuseppantonio Di Franco, F. Galeazzi & V. Vassallo, eds. *Authenticity and Cultural Heritage in the Age of 3D Digital Reproductions.* Cambridge: McDonald Institute for Archaeological Research, pp. 49–56.

Jeffrey, S., Hale, A., Jones, C., Jones, S., & Maxwell, M. (2015). The ACCORD Project : archaeological community co-production of research resources. In F. Giligny, F. Djindjian, L. Costa, P. Moscati & S. Robert, eds. *CAA2014 21st Century Archaeology: Concepts, Methods, and Tools. Proceedings of the 42nd Annual Conference on Computer Applications and Quantitative Methods in Archaeology.* Oxford: Archeopress, pp. 289–95.

Jensen, P. (2018a). Semantically enhanced 3D: a web-based platform for spatial integration of excavation documentation at Alken Enge, Denmark. *Journal of Field Archaeology* 43(sup1), S31–S44.

Jensen, P. (2018b). Evaluating authenticity: the authenticity of 3D models in archaeological field documentation. In P. Di Giuseppantonio Di Franco, F. Galeazzi & V. Vassallo, eds. *Authenticity and Cultural Heritage in the Age of 3D Digital Reproductions.* Cambridge: McDonald Institute for Archaeological Research, pp. 59–74.

Jones, S. (2010). Negotiating authentic objects and authentic selves: beyond the deconstruction of authenticity. *Journal of Material Culture* 15, 181–203.

Jones, S., Jeffrey, S. Maxwell, S. & Hale, M. (2018). 3D heritage visualization and the negotiation of authenticity: the ACCORD project. *International Journal of Heritage Studies* 1–21.

Jones, S. & Yarrow, T. (2013). Crafting authenticity: an ethnography of conservation practice. *Journal of Material Culture* 18(1), 3–26.

Joy, J. & Elliot, M. (2018). Cast aside or case in a new light? The Maudslay replica Maya cast at the Museum of Archaeology and Anthropology, Cambridge. In P. Di Giuseppantonio Di Franco, F. Galeazzi & V. Vassallo, eds. *Authenticity and Cultural Heritage in the Age of 3D Digital Reproductions*. Cambridge: McDonald Institute for Archaeological Research, pp. 13–24.

Kansa, E. (2012). Openness and archaeology's information ecosystem. *World Archaeology* 44(4), 498–520.

Kansa, E. (2014). Open context and linked data. *ISAW Papers* 7.10. http://dlib .nyu.edu/awdl/isaw/isaw-papers/7/kansa

Kersel, M. (2016). Response: living a semi-digital kinda life. In E. Averett, J. Gordon & D. Counts, eds. *Mobilizing the Past for a Digital Future: The Potential of Digital Archaeology*. Grand Forks: Digital Press, University of North Dakota. pp.475–92.

Kersten, T. P. & Lindstaedt, M. (2012). Image-based low-cost systems for automatic 3D recording and modelling of archaeological finds and objects. In M. Loannides, D. Fritsch, J. Leissner, R. Davies, F. Remondino & R. Caffo, eds. *Progress in Cultural Heritage Preservation: 4th International Conference, EuroMed 2012, Lemessos, Cyprus, October 29–November 3, 2012, Proceedings*. Vol. 7616. Springer Science & Business Media, pp. 1–10.

Khunti, R. (2018). The problem with printing Palmyra: exploring the ethics of using 3D printing technology to reconstruct heritage. *Studies in Digital Heritage* 2(1).

Koller, D. (2008). Virtual archaeology and computer-aided reconstruction of the Severan Marble Plan. In B. Frischer & A. Dakour-Hild, eds. *Beyond Illustration: 2D and 3D Digital Technologies as Tools for Discovery in Archaeology*. Archaeopress, pp. 125–33.

Kotoula, E. (2016). Reflectance Transformation Imaging beyond the visible: ultraviolet reflected and ultraviolet induced visible. In S. Campana, R. Scopigno, G. Carpentiero & M. Cirillio, eds. *CAA2015 Keep the Revolution Going. Proceedings of the 43rd Annual Conference on Computer Applications and Quantitative Methods in Archaeology*. Archeopress, pp. 909–18.

Kotoula, E. & Earl, G. (2015). Integrated RTI approaches for the study of painted surfaces. In F. Giligny, F. Djindjian, L. Costa, P. Moscati &

S. Robert, eds. *CAA2014 21st Century Archaeology: Concepts, Methods, and Tools. Proceedings of the 42nd Annual Conference on Computer Applications and Quantitative Methods in Archaeology.* Archeopress, pp. 123–34.

Laharnar, B., Lozić, E. & Štular, B. (2019). A structured Iron Age landscape in the hinterland of Knežak, Slovenia. In D. C. Cowley, M. Fernández-Götz, T. Romankiewicz & H. Wendling, eds. *Rural Settlement. Relating Buildings, Landscape, and People in the European Iron Age.* Leiden, Sidestone Press.

Lake, M. (2012). Open archaeology. *World Archaeology* 44(4), 471–78.

Lami, M. R., Opgenhaffen, L. & Kisjes, I. (2016). Pottery goes digital. 3D laser scanning technology and the study of archaeological ceramics. In S. Campana, R. Scopigno, G. Carpentiero & M. Cirillio, eds. *CAA2015 Keep the Revolution Going. Proceedings of the 43rd Annual Conference on Computer Applications and Quantitative Methods in Archaeology.* Archeopress, pp. 909–18.

Landeschi, G., Dell'Unto, N., Ferdani, D., Lindgren, S., & Leander Touati, A.-M. (2015). Enhanced 3D-GIS: documenting insula V 1 in Pompeii. In F. Giligny, F. Djindjian, L. Costa, P. Moscati & S. Robert, eds. *CAA2014 21st Century Archaeology: Concepts, Methods, and Tools. Proceedings of the 42nd Annual Conference on Computer Applications and Quantitative Methods in Archaeology.* Archeopress, pp. 349–60.

Leighton, M. (2015). Excavation methodologies and labour as epistemic concerns in the practices of archaeology. Comparing examples from British and Andean archaeology. *Archaeological Dialogues* 22(1), 65–88.

Lercari, N. (2016). Terrestrial laser scanning in the age of sensing. In M. Forte & S. Campana, eds. *Digital Methods and Remote Sensing in Archaeology.* Springer, pp. 3–34.

Lock, G. (2003). *Using Computers in Archaeology: Towards Virtual Pasts.* London, Routledge.

López, M., de Haro, F. A., Lara, L. S. et al. (2016). Cástulo in the 21st century: a test site for a new digital information system. In E. Averett, J. Gordon & D. Counts, eds. *Mobilizing the Past for a Digital Future: The Potential of Digital Archaeology.* Grand Forks: Digital Press, University of North Dakota, pp. 319–36.

Löwenborg, D. (2018). Knowledge production with data from archaeological excavations. In I. Huvila, ed. *Archaeology and Archaeological Information in the Digital Society.* London, Routledge, pp. 37–53.

Lycett, S. J. & von Cramon-Taubadel, N. (2013). A 3D morphometric analysis of surface geometry in Levallois cores: patterns of stability and variability across regions and their implications. *Journal of Archaeological Science* 40(3), 1508–17.

Malzbender, T., Gelb, D. & Wolters, H. (2001). Polynomial Texture Maps. In *SIGGRAPH '01: Proceedings of the 28th Annual Conference on Computer Graphics and Interactive Techniques*, New York: ACM, pp. 519–52.

Mara, H. & Bogacz, B. (2016). A bridge to digital humanities: geometric methods and machine learning for analysing ancient script in 3D. In S. Campana, R. Scopigno, G. Carpentiero & M. Cirillio, eds. *CAA2015 Keep the Revolution Going. Proceedings of the 43rd Annual Conference on Computer Applications and Quantitative Methods in Archaeology.* Archeopress, pp. 889–98.

McCoy, M. (2017). Geospatial big data and archaeology: prospects and problems too great to ignore. *Journal of Archaeological Science* 84, 74–94.

Merchán, P., Salamanca, S. &Adán, A. (2011). Restitution of sculptural groups using 3D scanners. *Sensors* 11, 8497–518.

Mickel, A. (2020). The proximity of communities to the expanse of big data. *Journal of Field Archaeology* 45(Sup 1), S51–S60.

Mlekuž, D. (2013). Messy landscapes: lidar and the practices of landscaping. In R. S. Opitz & D. C. Cowley, eds. *Interpreting Archaeological Topography: 3D Data, Visualisation and Observation.* Oxford: Oxbow Books, pp. 88–99.

Morgan, C. & Eve, S. (2012). DIY and digital archaeology: what are you doing to participate? *World Archaeology* 44(4), 521–37.

Morgan, C. & Winter, J (2015). Introduction: critical blogging in archaeology. *Internet Archaeology* 39. https://doi.org/10.11141/ia.39.11

Morgan, C. & Wright, H. (2018). Pencils and pixels: drawing and digital media in archaeological field recording. *Journal of Field Archaeology* 43(2), 136–51.

Moscati, P. (2019). Informatica archeologica e archeologia digitale le risposte dalla rete. *Archeologia e Calcolatori*, 30, 21–38.

Moshenska, G. (2017). Introduction: public archaeology as practice and scholarship where archaeology meets the world. In G. Moshenska, ed. *Key Concepts in Public Archaeology.* London: UCL Press. pp. 1–13.

Motz, C. (2016). Sangro Valley and the five (paperless) seasons: lessons on building effective digital recording workflows for archaeological fieldwork. In E. Averett, J. Gordon & D. Counts, eds. *Mobilizing the Past for a Digital Future: The Potential of Digital Archaeology.* Grand Forks: Digital Press, University of North Dakota. pp. 77–110.

Motz, C. F & Carrier, S. (2013). Paperless recording at the Sangro Valley Project. In G. Earl, T. Sly, A. Chrysanthi, P. Murrieta-Flores, C. Papadopoulos,

I. Romanowska & D. Wheatley, eds., *Archaeology in the Digital Era: Papers from the 40th Annual Conference of Computer Applications and Quantitative Methods in Archaeology (CAA), Southampton, 26–29 March 2012.* Amsterdam: Amsterdam University Press, pp. 25–30.

Oikarinen, T. (2016). Utilisation of a game engine for archaeological visualization. In S. Campana, R. Scopigno, G. Carpentiero & M. Cirillio, eds. *CAA2015 Keep the Revolution Going. Proceedings of the 43rd Annual Conference on Computer Applications and Quantitative Methods in Archaeology.* Archeopress, pp. 27–34.

Olson, B. R. & Caraher, W. R., eds. (2015). *3D Imaging in Mediterranean Archaeology.* Grand Forks, ND: The Digital Press.

Olson, B. R., Placchetti, R. A., Quartermaine, J. & Killebrew, A. E. (2013). The Tel Akko Total Archaeology Project (Akko, Israel): assessing the suitability of multi-scale 3D field recording in archaeology. *Journal of Field Archaeology* 38, 244–62.

Opitz, R. (2013). An overview of airborne and terrestrial laser scanning in archaeology. In R. S. Opitz & D. C. Cowley, eds. *Interpreting Archaeological Topography: 3D Data, Visualisation and Observation.* Oxford: Oxbow Books, pp. 13–31.

Opitz, R. (2015). Three dimensional field recording in archaeology: an example from Gabii. In B. Olson & W. Caraher, eds. *Visions of Substance: 3D Imaging in Mediterranean Archaeology.* Grand Forks: Digital Press, University of North Dakota, pp. 73–86.

Opitz, R. (2018). Publishing archaeological excavation at the digital turn. *Journal of Field Archaeology* 43(Sup 1), S68–S82.

Opitz, R. S. & Cowley, D. C., eds. (2013a) *Interpreting Archaeological Topography: 3D Data, Visualisation and Observation.* Oxford: Oxbow Books.

Opitz, R. S. & Cowley, D. C. (2013b). Interpreting archaeological topography: lasers, 3D data, observation, visualization and application. In R. S. Opitz & D. C. Cowley, eds. *Interpreting Archaeological Topography: 3D Data, Visualisation and Observation.* Oxford: Oxbow Books, pp. 1–12.

Opitz, R., Mogetta, M. & Terrenato, N. (2016). *A Mid-Republican House from Gabii.* Ann Arbor: University of Michigan Press.

Orton, D., Gaastra, J. & Linden, M. V. (2016). Between the Danube and the deep blue sea: zooarchaeological meta-analysis reveals variability in the spread and development of Neolithic farming across the western Balkans. *Open Quaternary* 2, Art. 6.

Palma, G., Siotto, E., Proesmans, M., Baldassari, M., Batino, S. & Scopigno, R. (2013). Telling the story of ancient coins by means of interactive RTI images visualization. In G. Earl, T. Sly, A. Chrysanti, P. Murrieta-Flores, C. Papadopoulos, I. Romanowska & D. Wheatley, eds. *Archaeology in the Digital Era. Papers from the 40th Annual Conference of Computer Applications and Quantitative Methods in Archaeology, Southampton.* Amsterdam: Amsterdam University Press, pp. 177–85

Papadopoulos, C., Hamilakis, Y., Kyparissi-Apostolika, N. & Díaz-Guardamino, M. (2019). Digital sensoriality: the neolithic figurines from Koutroulou Magoula, Greece. *Cambridge Archaeological Journal* 29(4), 625–52.

Perry, S. (2019). The enchantment of the archaeological record. *European Journal of Archaeology* 22(3), 354–71.

Perry, S. & Beale, N. (2015). The social web and archaeology's restructuring: impact, exploitation, disciplinary change. *Open Archaeology* 1, 153–65.

Perry, S., Shipley, L. & Osborne, J. (2015). Digital media, power and (in) equality in archaeology and heritage. *Internet Archaeology* 38. https://doi.org/10.11141/ia.38.4

Petersson, B. & Larsson, C. (2018). From storing to storytelling – archaeological museums and digitization. Huvila, I., ed. *Archaeology and Archaeological Information in the Digital Society.* London, Routledge, pp. 70–105.

Petri, G. (2014). The public domain vs. the museum: the limits of copyright and reporductions of two-dimensional works of art. *Journal of Conservation and Museum Studies* 12(1), 1–12.

Pfarr-Harfst, M. (2015). 25 years of experience in virtual reconstructions – research projects, status quo of current research and visions for the future. In F. Giligny, F. Djindjian, L. Costa, P. Moscati & S. Robert, eds. *CAA2014 21st Century Archaeology: Concepts, Methods, and Tools. Proceedings of the 42nd Annual Conference on Computer Applications and Quantitative Methods in Archaeology.* Archeopress, pp. 585–92.

Piccoli, C. (2016). Enhancing GIS urban data with the 3rd Dimension: a procedural modelling approach. In S. Campana, R. Scopigno, G. Carpentiero & M. Cirillio, eds. *CAA2015 Keep the Revolution Going. Proceedings of the 43rd Annual Conference on Computer Applications and Quantitative Methods in Archaeology.* Archeopress, pp. 815–24.

Pietroni, E. (2016). From remote to embodied sensing: new perspectives for virtual museums and archaeological landscape communication. In M. Forte & S. Campana, eds. *Digital Methods and Remote Sensing in Archaeology.* Springer, pp. 437–74.

Pires, H., Ortiz, P., Marques, P. & Sanchez, H. (2006). Close-range Laser Scanning Applied to Archaeological Artifacts Documentation. Virtual

Reconstruction of an XVIth Century Ceramic Pot. In M. Ioannides, D. Arnold, F. Niccolucci & K. Mania, eds. *The 7th International Symposium on Virtual Reality, Archaeology and Cultural Heritage VAST.*

Potenziani, M., Callieri, M., Dellepiane, M., Corsini, M., Ponchio, F. & Scopigno, R. (2015). 3DHOP: 3D heritage online presenter. *Computers & Graphics* (52), 129–41.

Powlesland, D. (2016). 3Di – Enhancing the record, extending the returns, 3D imaging from free range photography and its application during excavation. In H. Kamermans, W. de Neef, C. Piccoli, A. G. Poluschny & R. Scopigno., eds. *The Three Dimensions of Archaeology (Proceedings of the XVII UISPP World Congress (1–7 September 2014, Burgos, Spain).* Oxford: Archaeopress, pp. 13–32.

Quartermaine, J., Olson, B. R. & Killebrew, A. E. (2014), Image-based modeling approaches to 2D and 3D digital drafting in archaeology at Tel Akko and Qasrin: two case studies. *Journal of Eastern Mediterranean Archaeology and Heritage Studies* 2, 110–27.

Rabinowitz, A. (2015). The work of archaeology in the age of digital surrogacy. In B. Olson & W. Caraher, eds. *Visions of Substance: 3D Imaging in Mediterranean Archaeology.* Grand Forks, ND: The Digital Press at the University of North Dakota. pp. 27–42.

Reilly, P. (1991). Towards a Virtual Archaeology. In S. Rahtz & K. Lockyear, eds. *CAA90. Computer Applications and Quantitative Methods in Archaeology 1990* (BAR International Series 565). Oxford: Tempus Reparatum, pp. 132–39.

Reinhard, A. (2016). *Archaeogaming: An Introduction to Archaeology in and of Video Games.* New York: Berghahn Books.

Remondino, F. (2014). Photogrammetry – Basic Theory. In F. Remondion & S. Campana, eds. *3D Recording and Modelling in Archaeology and Cultural Heritage: Theory and Best Practices.* BAR International Series 2598. Oxford: Archeopress, pp. 63–72.

Remondino, F. & El-Hakim, S. (2006). Image-based 3D modelling: a review. *The Photogrammetric Record* 21(115), 269–91.

Richards, J. D. & Niccolucci, F., eds. (2019). *The ARIADNE Impact.* Budapest: Archaeolingua.

Richards, J. D. & Ryan, N. S. (1985). *Data Processing in Archaeology.* Cambridge: Cambridge University Press.

Richardson, E., Grosman, L., Smilansky, U. & Werman, M. (2012). Extracting scar and ridge features from 3D-scanned lithic artifacts. In G. Earl, T. Sly, A. Chrysanthi, P. Murrieta-Flores, C. Papadopoulos, I. Romanowska & D. Wheatley, eds., *Archaeology in the Digital Era: Papers from the 40th*

Annual Conference of Computer Applications and Quantitative Methods in Archaeology (CAA), Southampton, 26–29 March 2012. Amsterdam: Amsterdam University Press, pp. 83–92.

Richardson, L.-J. (2013). A digital public archaeology? *Papers from the Institute of Archaeology* 32(1), 1–12.

Richardson, L.-J. (2015). Micro-blogging and online community. *Internet Archaeology* 39. https://doi.org/10.11141/ia.39.2

Richardson, L.-J. (2018). Ethical challenges in digital public archaeology. *Journal of Computer Applications in Archaeology* 1(1), 64–73.

Richardson, L.-J. (2019). Using social media as a source for understanding public perceptions of archaeology: research challenges and methodological pitfalls. *Journal of Computer Applications in Archaeology* 2(1), 151–62.

Richardson, L.-J. & Booth, T. (2017). Response to 'Brexit, Archaeology and Heritage: Reflections and Agendas.' Papers from the Institute of Archaeology 27(1): 1–5.

Risbøl, O. (2013). Cultivating the 'wilderness' – how lidar can improve archaeological landscape understanding. In R. S. Opitz & D. C. Cowley, eds. *Interpreting Archaeological Topography: 3D Data, Visualisation and Observation*. Oxford: Oxbow Books, pp. 51–62.

Roosevelt, C. H., Cobb, P., Moss, E., Olson, B. R. & Ünlüsoy, S. (2015). Excavation is digitization: advances in archaeological practice. *Journal of Field Archaeology* 40, 325–46.

Sammons, J. F. D. (2018). Application of Reflectance Transformation Imaging (RTI) to the study of ancient graffiti from Herculaneum, Italy. *Journal of Archaeological Science: Reports* 17, 184–94.

Sapirstein, P. (2016). Accurate measurement with photogrammetry at large sites. *Journal of Archaeological Science* 66, 137–45.

Sapirstein, P. (2018). A high-precision photogrammetric recording system for small artifacts. *Journal of Cultural Heritage* 31, 33–45.

Sapirstein, P. & Murray, S. (2017). Establishing best practices for photogrammetric recording during archaeological fieldwork. *Journal of Field Archaeology* 42, 337–50.

Sayer, F. (2014). Politics and the development of community archaeology in the UK. *The Historic Environment* 5(1), 55–73.

Scholtz, S. & Chenhall, R. G. (1976). Archaeological data banks in theory and practice. *American Antiquity* 41(1), 89–96.

Seitsonen, O. (2017). Crowdsourcing cultural heritage: public participation and conflict legacy in Finland. *Journal of Community Archaeology and Heritage* 4(2), 115–30.

Shaw, R., Rabinowitz, A. & Golden, P. (2018). A deep gazetter of time periods. DH 2018. https://dh2018.adho.org/en/a-deep-gazetteer-of-time-periods

Sikora, J. & Kittel, P. (2018). Closing a gap with a simple toy: how the use of the tablet affected the documentation workflow during the excavations of the Rozprza Ring-Fort (Central Poland). In M. Matsumoto & E. Uleberg, eds. *CAA2016: Oceans of Data. Proceedings of the 44th Conference on the Computer Applications and Quantitative Methods in Archaeology.* Oxford: Archaeopress.

Smith, N. G., Beale, G., Richards, J. & Scholma-Mason, N. (2018). Maeshowe: the application of RTI to Norse Runes. *Internet Archaeology* 47. https://doi .org/10.11141/ia.47.8

Smith, N. G. & Levy, T. E. (2012). Real-Time 3D archaeological field recording: ArchField, an open-source GIS system pioneered in Southern Jordan. *Antiquity* 85:331.

Smith, N. G., Passone, L., Al-Said, S., Al-Farhan, M. & Levy, T. E. (2014). Drones in archaeology: integrated data capture, processing, and dissemination in the al-Ula Valley, Saudi Arabia. *Near Eastern Archaeology* 77:176–81.

Sobotkova, A., Ross, S. A., Ballsun-Stanton, B. et al. (2016). Measure twice, cut once: cooperative deployment of a generalized, archaeology-specific field data collection system. In E. Averett, J. Gordon & D. Counts, eds. *Mobilizing the Past for a Digital Future: The Potential of Digital Archaeology.* Grand Forks: Digital Press, University of North Dakota, pp. 337–72.

Štuhec, S. &. Zachar, J. (2017). Digital photogrammetry. In Zachar, J., M. Horňák & P. Novaković, eds. *3D Digital Recording of Archaeological, Architectural and Artistic Heritage.* CONPRA Series, Vol. 1. Ljubljana: University of Ljubljana Press, Faculty of Arts. pp. 33–52.

Stúlar, B. (forthcoming). Scientific dissemination of archaeological interpretation of airborne LiDAR-derived data: a manifesto. In K. Garstki, ed. *Critical Archaeology in the Digital Age.* The Cotsen Institute of Archaeology Press.

Štular, B. & Štuhec, S. (2015). *3D Archaeology: Early Medieval Earrings from Kranj.* Ljubljana: ZRC SAZU, Institute of Archaeology and ZRC Publishing.

Tasić, N. (2017a) About digital field documentation. In N. Tasić, P. Novaković, M. Horňák, eds. *Virtual Reconstructions and Computer Visualisations in Archaeological Practice, CONPRA Series, Vol. IV.* Ljubljana: University of Ljubljana Press, Faculty of Arts, pp. 23-25.

Tasić, N. (2017b). Augmented reality as an output. In N. Tasić, P. Novaković, M. Horňák, eds. *Virtual Reconstructions and Computer Visualisations in Archaeological Practice, CONPRA Series, Vol. IV.* Ljubljana: University of Ljubljana Press, Faculty of Arts, pp. 79–86.

Taylor, J. S., Issavi, J., Berggren, Å. , Lukas, D., Mazzucato, C., Tung, B. & Dell'Unto, N. (2018). 'The rise of the machine': the impact of digital tablet recording in the field at Çatalhöyük. *Internet Archaeology*, 47. https://doi.org /10.11141/ia.47.1

Thomas, D. H. (1978). The awful truth about statistics in archaeology. *American Antiquity* 43(2), 231–44.

Thomas, S. (2017). Community archaeology. In G. Moshenska, ed. *Key Concepts in Public Archaeology*. London: UCL Press, pp. 14–30.

Trier, Ø. D., Cowley, D. C. & Waldeland, A. U. (2019). Using deep neural networks on airborne laser scanning data: results from a case study of semi-automatic mapping of archaeological topography on Arran, Scotland. *Archaeological Prospection* 26, 165–75.

Tronchère, H., Bouvard, E., Mor, S., Fernagu, A. & Ramona, J. (2016). From the excavation to the scale model: a digital approach. In S. Campana, R. Scopigno, G. Carpentiero & M. Cirillio, eds. *CAA2015 Keep the Revolution Going. Proceedings of the 43rd Annual Conference on Computer Applications and Quantitative Methods in Archaeology*. Oxford: Archeopress. pp. 3–10.

Unger, J., Hemker, C., Lobinger, C. & Jan, M. (2020). VirtualArch: making archaeological heritage visible. *Internet Archaeology* 54. https://doi.org/10 .11141/ia.54.2

Verschoof-van der Vaart, W. B. & Lambers, K. (2019). Learning to look at LiDAR: the use of R-CNN in the automated detection archaeological objects in LiDAR data from the Netherlands. *Journal of Computer Application in Archaeology* 2(1), 31–40.

VanValkenburgh, P. & Dufton, J. A. (2020). Big archaeology: horizons and blindspots. *Journal of Field Archaeology* 45(Sup 1), S1–S7.

Vince, A. (1996). Editorial. *Internet Archaeology* 1. https://doi.org/10.11141 /ia.1.7

Walker, D. (2014). Antisocial media in archaeology? *Archaeological Dialogues* 21(2), 217–35. https://doi.org/10.1017/S1380203814000221

Walldrodt, J. (2016). Why paperless: technology and changes in archaeological practice, 1996–2016. In E. Averett, J. Gordon & D. Counts, eds. *Mobilizing the Past for a Digital Future: The Potential of Digital Archaeology*. Grand Forks: Digital Press, University of North Dakota, pp. 33–50.

Watrall, E. (2016). Archaeology, the digital humanities, and the 'Big Tent'. In M. K. Gold & L. F. Klein, eds. *Debate in the Digital Humanities*. Minneapolis: University of Minnesota Press.

Wernke, S. A., Hernández, C., Marcone, G., Oré, G., Rodriquez, A. & Traslaviña, A. (2016). Beyond the basemap: multiscalar survey through aerial photogrammetry in the Andes. In E. Averett, J. Gordon & D. Counts, eds. *Mobilizing the Past for a Digital Future: The Potential of Digital Archaeology.* Grand Forks: Digital Press, University of North Dakota, pp. 251–78.

Wheeler, M. (1954). *Archaeology from the Earth.* Oxford: Clarendon Press.

Wihelmson, H. & Dell'Unto, N. (2015). Virtual taphonomy: a new method integrating excavation and postprocessing in an archaeological context. *American Journal of Physical Anthropology* 157, 305–21.

Wilkinson, M. D., Dumontier, M., Aalbersberg, I. J., Appleton, G., Axton, M., Baak, A., Blomberg, N., Boiten, J. W., da Silva Santos, L. B., Bourne, P.E. & Bouwman, J. (2016). The FAIR Guiding Principles for scientific data management and stewardship. *Scientific data*, 3. https://doi.org/10.1038/sdata.2016.18

Witmore, C. L. (2009). Prolegomena to open pasts: on archaeological memory practices. *Archaeologies: Journal of the World Archaeological Congress* 5 (3), 511–45.

Yates, D. (2018). Crowdsourcing antiquities crime fighting: a review of GlobalXplorer. *Advances in Archaeological Practice* 6(2), 173–78.

Zachar, J. & Horňák, M. (2017). 3D recording in archaeological practice. In Zachar, J., M. Horňák & P. Novaković, eds. *3D Digital Recording of Archaeological, Architectural and Artistic Heritage.* CONPRA Series, Vol. 1. Ljubljana: University of Ljubljana Press, Faculty of Arts.

Zachar, J. & Štuhec, S. (2015). Old versus new – introducing image-based 3D modeling into the general documentation workflow of archaeological rescue excavations. Case studies: the Čachtice and Bratislava castles, Slovakia. In F. Giligny, F. Djindjian, L. Costa, P. Moscati & S. Robert, eds. *CAA2014 21st Century Archaeology: Concepts, Methods, and Tools. Proceedings of the 42nd Annual Conference on Computer Applications and Quantitative Methods in Archaeology.* Archeopress, pp. 529-530.

Acknowledgements

I must thank Bettina Arnold and Manuel Fernàndez-Götz for the invitation to contribute to this ambitious series. I am indebted to the two reviewers whose extensive comments significantly strengthened the piece, filling in gaps in content and coverage. I must also thank Adrienne Frie for reading and commenting on drafts of this text, whose eye for detail is always a welcome contribution and whose strength during a pandemic supported me in the writing process. Finally, thanks are due to Derek Counts, Erin Averett, and Michael Toumazou for their friendship and collaboration over the last decade. Any errors or content biases remain my own and do not reflect the enormous scope of this subject.

I would like to dedicate this Element to my students at Marquette University, University at Buffalo, and University of Wisconsin–Milwaukee who challenged, contributed, and reframed many of the ideas that eventually made their way into this Element.

Cambridge Elements $\equiv$

The Archaeology of Europe

Manuel Fernández-Götz
University of Edinburgh

Manuel Fernández-Götz is Reader in European Archaeology and Head of the Archaeology Department **at** the University of Edinburgh. In 2016 he was awarded the prestigious Philip Leverhulme Prize. His main research interests are Iron Age and Roman archaeology, social identities and conflict archaeology. He has directed fieldwork projects in Spain, Germany, the United Kingdom and Croatia.

Bettina Arnold
University of Wisconsin-Milwaukee

Bettina Arnold is a Full Professor of Anthropology at the University of Wisconsin-Milwaukee and Adjunct Curator of European Archaeology at the Milwaukee Public Museum. Her research interests include the archaeology of alcohol, the archaeology of gender, mortuary archaeology, Iron Age Europe and the history of archaeology.

About the Series

Elements in the Archaeology of Europe is a collaborative publishing venture between Cambridge University Press and the European Association of Archaeologists. Composed of concise, authoritative, and peer-reviewed studies by leading scholars, each volume in this series will provide timely, accurate, and accessible information about the latest research into the archaeology of Europe from the Paleolithic era to the end of antiquity, as well as on heritage preservation.

E
A   European Association
A   *of* Archaeologists

Cambridge Elements ☰

The Archaeology of Europe

Elements in the Series